WHAT PEOPLE ARE S
FLIP THE SW...

Joan is an incredible entrepreneur who truly understands the direction digital business is headed. Watching her lead thousands of people towards better lives in this digital revolution is nothing short of remarkable. Her words are backed by years of experience, passions and intelligence. Listen carefully.

> DARREN BIRKS
> **Digital Entrepreneur**

Joan's vulnerability is such an inspiration! This book will inspire you to find your own truth and guide you through the journey of transforming your life into one that you love through all the good and bad. I felt like Joan was holding my hand every step of the way as she guides the reader through her own life and shares life-changing techniques.

> GINNA TASSANELLI
> **Business, Personal Brand, & Image Consultant**

Joan's new book, Flip The Switch, is full of practical advice and methods to help you reframe your life. We all know what we "should" do but often get trapped in patterns of thinking and behaviors that make change hard. Joan has personal experiences that she shares honestly and authentically. I'm so thankful she's shared her stories in this book to bring others along on her journey. If Joan can change, so can I!

> SUE BRADLEY
> **President, Keep The People, KTP Consulting Services**

This book is for anyone who is daring enough to make the changes necessary to live the life of their dreams! She shares practical wisdom, sound advice and simple activities that have worked for her and the thousands of individuals and teams she's worked with. She's brilliant, practical and inspiring. Flip The Switch is the perfect guide to show you the path to living your best life, too.

> KRISTI LUCARIELLO
> **Global Sales Training & Enablement, Blancco**

Joan's years of experience as a successful leader and coach has given her insight to what it takes to be outstanding in this profession. Her book breaks down simple thoughts and action steps to take your business to the next level and live a more fulfilling life. Enjoy the book and share it - you will impact lives!

NICKI KEOHOHOU
Co-Founder and CEO of the Direct Selling World Alliance

Recommending Joan to be your coach is the easy part. All you have to do is be willing to change and she will empower you with the tools to do it!

BRIAN NILSEN
Founder, Circuit of Northwest

The simple, yet profound wisdom that Joan brings to you through her teachings will transform your life at a soul level. Whether you came here looking for business training, self-help, or a mindset shift, you will leave feeling like you have a new friend guiding you in areas you didn't even realize needed it!

DANI FRYER
Online Entrepreneur, Intuitive Coach, Reiki Healer

Joan Robison is sharing her personal formula for success. A formula that works! She is a visionary and a leader who knows how to motivate and share concepts in an easy readable way. The answers are all here in this influential book with one powerful message: You, too, can flip the switch.

MARY DELANEY, PHD
Psychologist

A real gem!! This book is a must have for any entrepreneur looking to overcome limiting beliefs and positivity impact outcomes! Joan's simple way of breaking down proven strategies will have your business and your life soaring!

SARAH NILSEN
VP of Sales, Green Compass

Flip The Switch is the opportunity of a lifetime to be mentored by Joan Robison. She was my very first business mentor and helped me break through some patterns that were holding me back. While I read this incredible book, it took me back to that time where I had her voice in my ear, guiding me to step into my greatness. Do yourself a favor and devour this book!

Dr. Dana McGrady
Doctor of Oriental Medicine, Better Health and Wellness Center

I can think of no one more qualified to write a book like Flip The Switch than Joan Robison. I first met Joan when she was a top sales leader at a company that hired me to produce their national convention and have worked with her in many capacities in the 20 years since. Flip The Switch isn't just about successful selling, it's about successful living. Joan not only shares her professional experience and knowledge, she also shares her unique insights on human nature, mentorship, and creating joyful success. It's a "how to" book that everyone should read.

Dick Wilson

Joan Robison's coaching programs consistently get people unstuck and moving from where they are to where they want to be. Joan's coaching style, wisdom and honest feedback create remarkable results with her team and clients.

Melissa Soete
CEO, GreenLight Mindset

Mastery of mindset is the centerpiece of success in any area of life! Flip The Switch gives you the practical tools needed to master your mindset. I love how Joan brings in the topic of mindset awareness by focusing on the words we speak as well as the actions you can take to change your vibration. By knowing how to coach and lead yourself, you will then be able to coach and lead others to success.

Julie Lucky
Founder & Executive Director, MONAT

FLIP
THE
Switch

Daniella!!

Keep shining your
Light!!

FLIP
THE

Switch

IGNITE TRANSFORMATIONAL CHANGE.
LIVE A LIFE YOU LOVE.

FOREWORD BY ROB SPERRY

JOAN ROBISON

SUNKIST PUBLISHING

For ease of readability, this book includes gender-specific language in the female gender. The ideas in this book are meant for all readers, regardless of gender. There is no intention to exclude; rather, the intention is to include each person.

This book is a reference only. The information given here is designed to help you make informed decisions to improve the quality of your life, and is not a substitute for mental health treatment. If you suspect that you have a serious mental health problem, it is recommended that you seek competent medical help.

SUNKIST PUBLISHING

DEDICATION

It is with deep gratitude that I acknowledge
the greatest source of all, God.
My answer will always be … YES!

To my parents,
Wayne and Marcia Carslin & Roger and Becky Nilsen.
Your love and belief in me
will forever be etched in my soul.

TABLE OF Contents

FOREWORD

For the last four years, I have had the opportunity to speak and train in 18 different countries. I have coached top leaders from all over the world, and one of the most successful students that I get to work with on a daily basis is Joan Robison.

What makes Joan qualified to write a book and teach you how to create transformation in your life is her experience. She isn't some guru teaching you based on what she has heard, but she instead gives you real-life examples. The ability to learn how to learn is the greatest ability one can have. Joan breaks down the blueprint for you to live a life that you love. The strategies that Joan gives you will not only make you happier, but they are the blueprint for how to have more success in anything you choose.

Joan has a unique blend of being extremely caring and bold at the same time. *Flip The Switch* is going to be your new favorite book. By engaging in the principles from this book, you are in for an exciting transformation.

I know you will benefit from reading this book just as I did. In it you will find absolutely inspiring stories and strategies to ignite that transformational change to live a life you love.

- ROB SPERRY
6x Author and Public Speaker
www.robsperry.com

INTRODUCTION

I delight each day in seeing people
Flip The Switch,
moving closer to living a life they love.

- JOAN ROBISON

INTRODUCTION

It was November 2020. Between a contentious election and a world-wide pandemic, tensions were high and our country was divided. People all over our country were in fear. Feelings of uncertainty plagued nearly every human being on earth. Lives were shaken and lost. People were terrified. I wanted to help people but wondered, "What could I do?"

As I meditated one morning, God said, "I need your help. People are in fear, and you are not. You know how to get yourself out of fear quickly, and you know how to help people. You know what to do." I am not a stranger to hearing God's voice nudging me in ways that I could never predict. God uses willing people to reveal His character and His miraculous ways. God equips the least of us to show His magnificent power.

"I hear you," I said, then asked, "Just how am I going to do that?" I have had moments of digging in my heels and being too afraid to take action, even when I know that God is asking me to do something. It often takes time for me to process what I'm being asked to do. In the end my answer is always, "Yes." I know what I am here for.

The way I pray is simple. I talk with God as I would my best friend. I ask questions like, "God, you want me to help people. Give me some ideas. Send me the people you want me to help. Show me specifically what you want me to do. I'll do it." Within a day of my prayer, I was invited to a training workshop hosted by my friend, Toni Vanschoyck. Going into the workshop, I didn't know the topic. When I found out it was about writing a book, I thought, "Really?!"

I doubted I could do this. I thought, "Write a book? Come on!" It wasn't on my bucket list.

I came to the idea of writing a book kicking and screaming. Procrastination took over. I got busy with anything and everything before I reached acceptance. I knew I needed to trust blindly that God would see me through like He always does.

Once I accepted that I was writing a book to help people live a life they love, my ideas began to come together effortlessly. That's when I knew I was on the right path. In my mind I pictured how people must feel being in fear. I was seeing fear firsthand with many people I worked with. Fear is darkness. God is light. To help people out of fear, they need a simple way to walk into the light. To *flip the switch*.

"That's it," I thought. I could show people how they've been in the dark. I could share ideas about becoming more aware and taking personal responsibility. I could help people see that they have the power of choice and that they, too, could walk in the light. By sharing how to do this in an easy way, I could offer a beacon of hope. I could provide tools that have helped me and others to get out of fear.

While I was thinking about this book, I had been holding group mindset Zoom sessions for the previous two and half years. I had witnessed several women transform their lives by practicing the tools they learned in those sessions. It was as if those Zooms were my training ground for *flip the switch* moments. By the end of November, my groups had doubled and tripled in size. The groups provided a variety of tools and practices to support a stronger mindset, tools that I will share with you in this book.

I used to talk about "pivoting," the skill of changing direction as you move from a problem to a solution. What I felt I wanted to share was bigger than going from problem to solution; it was about getting out of fear and living a life of love. Whether we are working on business skills or daily life practices, everything is elevated when we are out of fear and walking in the light.

When we are walking in the light, we shine. We become like a magnet. We can be seen by others, and we attract others. We can't see in the dark, and our world can become small and self-consuming. When we *flip the switch*, the light comes on. We can see again, and our world becomes bigger. As we grow and expand, we offer more value to others. We all have daily opportunities to *flip the switch*. I see a world in which millions of people become more aware of their personal power and choose to live a life of love instead of a life of fear.

I have been in the network marketing industry for over twenty years, and I learned very quickly that if I wanted to lead like the leaders I saw at conferences, I knew I needed to work on myself. My first commitment to myself was to follow my company's success plan for 90 days. I wanted to give it my best effort. Like most people, I had fears. At times, those fears paralyzed me. Thankfully, though, I stayed the course. By following the success plan, I learned to master the basics of the business and remain true to my values and principles.

There were days when I was frustrated with myself. I would ask, "When am I ever going to get this?" God would remind me that my heart for helping people was still my greatest asset. I wasn't polished or perfect. I was willing to be seen as I was. I knew people appreciated real vulnerability more than a fixed-up version of success that they often saw on social media. By showing people that I was working on getting better one step at a time, I was shining a light on the path.

Much of what I will share with you in this book came from watching and learning from what other successful people did. My learning started as a young child, watching my Grandpa Carl and my dad run a store. I continued to learn at Nordstrom, where I followed the best salespeople and studied what they did. I continued to learn and grow as I entered the network marketing channel. I sought out "the greats" and found ways to learn from them and work with them. *Flip The Switch* is a culmination of what I have taken from my years of experience and from observing and working with others.

This book is presented in two segments. The first four chapters are about **Working on Yourself**. You will explore ways to become the best possible version of yourself. The book starts with my story and provides you with lessons that can help you on your journey of self-improvement. Going to work on myself has always interested me like nothing else. I have grown passionate and relentless in the pursuit of getting better. I have had my share of bumps, bruises, and scars. As you will discover, I have made decisions that I haven't been proud of. I have learned to dust myself off, step out, and try new approaches. I'll provide ideas to help you on your journey. We'll look at mindset. We'll look at fear. And we'll explore the power of prayer, love, and meditation.

As you overcome challenges within yourself, you will have a greater desire to share what you are learning with others. The last four chapters are about **Working with Others**. I will introduce concepts that will equip you to work with people in powerful ways. We'll start with a look at your heart for people. We'll explore how you communicate. We'll look at the practice of coaching and how coaching others can help you build the people around you.

We will also explore leadership and empowerment. My greatest joy over the past years has been to see the people I've been privileged to partner with transform in ways they didn't think was possible. The tears and triumph. Oh … the funny stories! The sweetness as people have risen to become more of who they are created to be. Isn't that what life is all about?

My deepest hope is that you will devour the chapters in this book. Throughout the pages, you will find questions for reflection that encourage you to pause and think about your life. You'll find recommended actions to help you convert the ideas into daily choices. I hope you mark up the pages, reflect deeply on the ideas shared, and do the work to ignite transformation in your life.

Whether you are a network marketer, a self-employed entrepreneur, a manager who wants to become a stronger leader, or someone who wants a better way to live, **Flip The Switch** is for you. The concepts in this book can be applied to all areas of your life. You may be amazed at how simple these tools really are. With consistent practice you will begin noticing your life shifting more and more toward the light. I am talking the "pinch yourself" kind of amazement. You may even hear yourself saying, "I love my life."

Are you ready? Isn't it time to stop living in fear? I invite you to *flip the switch*. Let's ignite transformational change. Start living a life you love.

PART ONE

WORKING ON YOURSELF

Personal success starts by working on yourself first. Your life gets better when you get better at being YOU!

- JOAN ROBISON

CHAPTER ONE

CLEAN IT UP, ONE THING AT A TIME

The secret of change is to focus all your energy not on fighting the old, but on building the new.

- SOCRATES

CLEAN IT UP, ONE THING AT A TIME

I have been blessed to work with many incredible people, partnering with them as they ignited transformational change in their lives. I don't take this responsibility lightly. In most of my coaching relationships, my clients start by focusing on their skills. We soon discover that much of what we work on is more about their heart condition, what I think of as an "inside job."

Most of us have things we must clean up before we can start living lives we love. Fear is the most common barrier to change. Feeling fear isn't something most of us welcome with open arms. In fact, fear is the biggest dream killer. If left unattended, it can hold us hostage. For some, fear lasts a lifetime. I understand the depths of fear. I have lived it. At the start of my career, I had to confront many of my own fears. I cleaned up areas of my life that absolutely needed to be changed, one thing at a time.

If your well-being is compromised and the relationships closest to you are suffering or holding you back from the life you want, they deserve a look. You are worth it. You get to decide what is best for you. Making a mess is always easier than cleaning it up. And with any mess, think about how good you'll feel once it's cleaned up. Hang on to that hope. Stay with me.

In this chapter, I will share some of my story with you. I will share some of the lessons that led to transformational change in my life. It is my deepest hope that these words, from my heart, will touch a place in your soul, and you will find the courage to address your own something and start living a life you love.

Awareness is the first step to identifying and solving a problem.

In 1985, medical research conducted at the University of Maryland School of Medicine showed how internal and external dialogue significantly affect our health. Numerous articles about the way we think report that the average person has about 60,000 to 80,000 thoughts per day. It is commonly reported that 80% are based in fear, and 95% of those thoughts are repetitive.

The majority of people spend their time thinking in fear then replaying their thoughts over and over. Many people don't even realize they're living in a fear-based state. Many accept their lives as a sentence, not knowing they have the power of choice to create the lives they want. For much of my early adult life, I wasn't getting what I wanted. My thoughts were focused on the wrong things. To live a life you love, you have to address your fears. It is vital that you feel good emotionally, spiritually, and physically.

Helping people overcome their fears is why I wrote **Flip The Switch**. The idea for this book came to me one night as I was praying and meditating. It was as if God was saying, "People are living in fear. You are not. You've had a lot of practice. You know how to get out of fear, and you know how to help people get out of fear." I paused. I thought about it and realized this was true. I continued to listen as God's voice encouraged me. "I need your help, Joan. Share it in a simple way. Help more people become aware. Show them how their light shines from the inside out, according to the condition of their hearts."

I wondered if I was hearing correctly. As I laid there, I thought about what a big responsibility this was. I felt my own fear of inadequacy rearing its ugly head. I thanked the fear for making me aware and sent that fear back where it came from. I knew without a doubt what God was empowering me to do. It didn't take me long to think: What is the opposite of living in fear? Living a life of love. YES, that was it. So simple.

I thought if I could help people become aware sooner and get un-stuck more quickly, they could begin to improve their lives one thing at a time and start living lives they loved. After all, that is how I did it myself.

Living in fear is living in the dark. Our world becomes small, and we become consumed with our own thoughts. Living in love is living in the light. We begin to see our lives open up and become bigger. We expand, and so does our world. *Flip The Switch*. YES! In this book, I will teach you some simple ways to go from living in the dark to living in the light. I will share ways to shine your light for others, as you were made to live.

Let me ask you this: What fears are you living with that hold you back from your dreams and goals? When your life doesn't feel right, it is a sign you aren't living in alignment with your true nature. Your subconscious might be telling you it is time for a change. It could be as simple as addressing something small that is nagging you. Or perhaps you're facing something more significant. Perhaps you are uncertain why your results aren't where you want them to be. There could be things you aren't even aware of that are causing you to live in the dark. This was true for me.

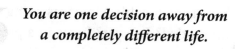

> *You are one decision away from*
> *a completely different life.*
>
> -MEL ROBBINS

The greatest gift doesn't always come with a pretty red bow.

I had spent an enjoyable evening with friends at a wine tasting dinner. I don't recall how much wine I consumed that evening because it was just a tasting. I do recall that as I got ready to leave I paused to assess how I was feeling. I was pretty sure I was fine. *"Just fine,"* I thought. I decided I would drink an extra bottle of water before leaving, telling myself it would surely make a difference. Alcohol has a way of altering reality. With my judgment impaired, I walked to my car and started my journey home.

Moments from my front door, my life changed drastically. I was about to turn into my driveway when I noticed red and blue lights flashing in my rear-view mirror. A moment later, I heard a siren. My heart sank then started pounding. I glanced to my right, and briefly felt the comfort of home. I gazed down the driveway and saw my porch light, offering a beacon of hope. I was home. Almost.

An officer came to my car window and asked for my license and registration. He asked me to step out of the car, lights still flashing, in front of my own home. After I performed a few ballet twirls, he said words that no one wants to hear: "Ms. Nilsen, you are under arrest. Anything you say can and will be used against you ..."

I had made the decision to drive after drinking, and it wasn't the first time. I wasn't sorry about drinking and driving; I was sorry I got caught. I took no responsibility for having created this entire scenario. I wanted to blame someone else for what was happening to me. That night, I blamed the police officer, wondering why he wasn't out arresting *real* criminals. My mind became cluttered with thoughts: I didn't have time for this. How was going to pay all these costs? Bail? Car impounded? Lawyer? I was in a place of justifying my actions while blaming others. I couldn't see the truth. It's hard to see when you are in the dark.

In a moment of clarity, I realized that in the past few months my drinking had been bothering me more and more. I knew I needed to address my drinking but didn't know how. I hoped for an easy way out. I even wished for a magic pill. The amount of time I spent thinking about how to take care of my problem, beating myself up, and justifying why I drank had begun consuming me. It was like a prison in the privacy of my mind. I had soul sickness, and the feeling wouldn't go away. Spirituality has always been a central element of my life, and I prayed. I asked for God's help. It didn't take me long that night to realize God was in full control, doing for me what I didn't have the strength to do on my own.

> *Be confident of this; he who began a good work in you will carry it on to completion.*
>
> -PHILIPPIANS 1:6

I clung to this Biblical promise. The light of God's spirit was starting to enter the cracks of my darkness. When I drank, my perception became distorted. Worse, I gave away my power to make good choices. Many of my choices caused unwanted drama, distraction, and an overall unhealthy well-being. In those days it didn't seem all that abnormal. After all, it was how I was living my life. My mind was consumed with the messes I made and cleaning them up. I spent too much time beating myself up, leaving little time for feeling good about myself.

I was awakening to the feelings I had suppressed. I was feeling things or emotions I had never allowed myself to feel. Through the process, I was starting to feel hopeful. I could see possibilities of a better life, free from the chains of alcohol. It was as if I was coming out of the dark. It was a flip of a switch duality moment. It was as if the switch had a dimmer feature. I was slowly awakening to a better way of life.

Owning my choices and taking responsibility.

I was booked into jail that evening and placed in a cell where I could see my reflection in a stainless-steel door. This was a defining moment. Some might call it an all-time low. I looked closely at myself and thought, "Wow. Just look at you. You got yourself into this. Now own it and do something about it." I can still picture myself looking around at my surroundings and wondering how I had ended up there. It caused me to think of how I wanted my life to be and that I was going about it all wrong. God was answering my prayers by placing that hopeful feeling in my heart.

I sat there alone with my thoughts. I imagined my son's little face. I loved him more than my own life. He thought the world of me, and I of him. We were a team. What was I doing? What kind of example was I showing him? That moment of clarity was one of my first driving forces. WHO did I want to be? What kind of mother did I want my son and daughters to see? I needed to make a change. I knew I needed help.

I was raised in a blended family. The older generation fought through problems and didn't talk about them. I see now that they were doing the best they could with the skills they had. When some of those family members gave up drinking, no one said much about it. When I thought about giving up drinking, I felt shame and guilt. I was hesitant to call my parents about my problem. I needed God's perspective.

I was not a stranger to having chats with God — nothing formal, just friendly or relational chats. I had moments of sobbing when I asked God, "Why am I doing these things? Why can't I get a grip on this?" My mind raced, and I couldn't seem to quiet the chatter. I felt such frustration with myself. I recall wishing my day would end and that I could stop thinking. Drinking wasn't working for me anymore. I wanted to sleep peacefully and start my day feeling good about myself. I asked the simplest prayer of all, "Help me."

That day was the start of a major flip of the switch in my life. Strange how a way out can be right in front of us and we don't see it. Then again, it's hard to see in the dark. I was awakening to the fact that my drinking had me in trapped in a never-ending cycle. I mustered up the courage to get the help I needed.

It is a strength to ask for help from God and others.

God answered my calls for help. As I sat in jail, I knew deep inside that I had a choice. I could have alcohol or I could have a life I loved. Both paths felt painful and scary. Not doing something about it was what I feared most. I physically felt impending doom. I feared losing everything I loved. There was a spark within me that told me I was destined for a better life. I had a deep desire to make my life something I was proud of, something worthwhile.

I was reminded of the stories in the Bible and in life when the power of God transformed circumstances and changed lives. Out of fear, out of darkness, into love, into the light. Faith is believing in the unseen. My faith was being stretched, and it required me to move beyond self-reliance. Terrified, I chose to get outside help. I realized I needed the fellowship of others who felt like me and understood me. I needed to heal the part of me that I was not dealing with, the part of me that wanted to escape and drink.

I was taking responsibility for myself and my actions, and it felt good. For the first time in a long time, my fear was met with an unusual sense of peace. I couldn't explain it. Today, I would call it confirmation that I was on the right path. I wanted desperately to feel good. I noticed that the more time I spent thinking about the life I wanted to create, the more freedom I felt. I could feel my soul awakening. One day at a time, living free from alcohol, my light began to shine. I got better, my life got better, and my world got bigger. I was experiencing a feeling I'd never experienced before. It felt so good. I loved feeling good. I was experiencing the full range of my emotions, and I was happier than I'd ever been.

God uses His people to shine His light.

As I look back, I recognize that what I needed appeared at exactly the right time. The people I needed were placed in my life. I remember conversations I'd had with a wise friend who owned a local restaurant. Years before, he had questioned his own drinking, and I wanted to talk with him. He always made time for me, and I had many lunches with him. I couldn't wait to hear what he had to say.

I had always noticed something was different about him. He had an especially kind way about him and a non-judgmental, matter-of-fact demeanor that drew me to him. I recall thinking, "This is exactly how I want people to feel about me." I always love a good story, and he had many. I also noticed he was successful in business and in life. He had a family and lived a life he loved. I wanted that kind of life, too.

Our chats touched the depths of my soul. He provoked my thoughts in a kind, curious way. No one likes to be told what to do, how to live, or what's right for them. It was obvious he knew this truth. He didn't lecture but instead gave me food for thought.

I asked him, "What was it that made you quit drinking?" He shared a few stories I could relate to, and we both laughed at the chaos drinking brought to people like us. He told me that when drinking just wasn't working for him anymore, he wanted more for his life. He said, "When you get sick and tired of being sick and tired, you'll do something about it. Not until." That stuck with me.

I thought, "How would this life of no drinking be possible for me?" It was more about whether I would be able to give up this love-hate relationship with drinking. I felt a physical fear like I was having an out-of-body experience, and it scared me. Drinking had become my comfort zone. What if I couldn't quit? I didn't want to fail.

Life isn't happening to me;
it's happening for me.

- ESTHER HICKS

Days and hours were revealing more clarity. It all made sense. God was meeting me where I was, orchestrating a plan every step of the way. I felt His presence gently, lovingly, leading me. My transformational change encompassed much more than not drinking. It was about my way of living. I was like a baby learning to walk. Change did not happen overnight. I needed to put one foot in front of the other and show up for my life. I was uncomfortable. By committing to one day at a time, I began finding comfort in the uncomfortable. I needed to be cleaned up to live a life I loved.

Thankfully, the desire to drink was being lifted. I was amazed. This is what I feared most. I was being called to a higher level of living. If I was going to lead people, I had to address this area of my life that was diminishing my self-esteem. I needed to take care of me before I could take care of others.

It took a while for me to acknowledge that I was grateful for the police officer that night. I know that he was doing his job to serve and protect. I was breaking the law. I never intended to hurt the people I loved, nor anyone else for that matter. Alcohol impaired my judgment, and that night was only one example. To be free of the hold alcohol had on me changed my life for the better. No one is exempt from challenges. I choose to look at challenges in a productive way and use them to strengthen myself.

We all have a monkey or two on our backs at one time or another. If there weren't things we had to work at, we would never grow. We would fold up like a house of cards. I look at times of growth as peeling back the layers, cleaning them up, and strengthening the foundation. One of the most difficult things a person will ever do is confront herself. I had many "warnings," and that night is what it took to get my attention. My options were glaringly obvious. It was as if God was making me feel repulsed by everything related to alcohol. I knew deep within that this was God's way of showing me He could change my feelings, too. I felt the assurance of God's strength and peace wash over me. I heard, "Trust me." That was enough.

Practice. Practice. Practice.

Think about a skill you have had to work at. Think of one that, no matter your natural ability, you had to practice. It could be learning a foreign language. You had to practice. It may be learning to play a musical instrument. You had to practice. For me, it was snow skiing. I remember the first few times I went skiing. It didn't matter that I wanted to be a good skier or even that I considered myself reasonably athletic. I had to practice. I had to fall and get back up again. I used practice to strengthen myself. Often, our greatest challenges become our assets when used to help and support others.

My dad used to say, "If you want to be good at something, you need to practice and always follow the best." I started skiing on the bunny hill. I got better with practice. I didn't feel comfortable for a time. In fact, it felt awkward. Eventually, with practice, I felt confident enough to take on a hill.

The same was true with cleaning up this area of my life. I had to practice. I had to be willing to be uncomfortable before I became comfortable. I had to follow someone who was walking the walk, free from alcohol, and do what she did. One day at a time, I found I could, too.

I continue to show up for life and practice being who I was created to be. I am not perfect. I just don't drink today. Tomorrow is another day, and it will take care of itself. Thankfully, like most habits, once you stop doing something, it has less hold on you. Once you address why you are doing something, the work and healing begin. I work a program that gives me a daily reprieve from alcohol based on my spiritual condition. I see God's hand at work in my life. I have free will, and each day I have a choice. I am so thankful that today I don't want to drink. Drinking has lost its luster. I never thought I'd be able to say that. My life is better because I **chose** a better way of living.

I know that many people have struggles like mine. Whether we have something more significant to clean up or something smaller, we all have areas of our lives that can hold us hostage from living lives we love.

For me, the way I felt was telling me to make a change. What I came to realize was that the majority of my problems increased dramatically when I was drinking. I used alcohol to escape pain and temporarily forget my problems. When I was drinking, I couldn't see that alcohol was actually making things worse. It took moments of clarity, free from drinking, to connect the dots.

I keep looking up and focusing on who I am becoming along the way. I know as long as I stay connected to God, I have a good chance of staying away from alcohol. One day at a time.

Our lives are filled with stories. I have shared one of mine with you in the hope that it will encourage you to think about your own. We all have challenges to overcome, whether large or small. Each challenge is an invitation to grow and become more of who we are meant to be. As I reflect on the personal growth that came from my challenges, these six lessons stand out:

Six Lessons:

1. **Awareness is the first step to understanding a problem.**
2. **Own your life by taking responsibility.**
3. **Ask for help.**
4. **Practice.**
5. **Choose between the pain of discipline or the pain of regret.**
6. **Focus on what you want to create in your life.**

Change is not easy. As I moved some of my life's darkest clouds out of the way to see the sunshine, I formed new habits. The habit I treasure most is to take regular breaks from day-to-day life so I can have conversations with myself. Yes, conversations with *myself*. My favorite way to inspire self-talk is to go for a walk and think about something I want in my life. I love to daydream. Other times, I pause with my favorite iced tea, a splash of lemonade, and fresh lemon. I think deeply about what is in my heart and on my mind. It is through these conversations that I can move in the direction of change.

In the pages that follow, we will look at how you can bring these lessons to your life. We will explore questions to think about in conversations with yourself. To get to the heart of what could be keeping you from living the live you love, let's dive into each of the six lessons.

Lesson 1: Awareness is the first step to understanding a problem.

Change can only happen when we become aware of what is keeping us in the dark. Transformation starts with a courageous and honest look at what is going inside us.

Ways to increase your self-awareness:

Pay attention to your feelings.

Sometimes we move from one scheduled event to the next without pausing to ask ourselves how we are feeling. Other times, we think about how others are feeling more than we think about our own emotions. We can't take care of others until we take care of ourselves. Give yourself permission to pay attention to YOU and to how YOU are feeling.

Meditate to quiet your mind.

Have you ever noticed how you can get more done when you work in an uncluttered space? Your mind works in a similar way. The practice of meditation quiets your mind from the clutter.

As you quiet your mind, you will feel more connected to yourself and God. You will experience greater perspective and awareness. I like to think of praying as me phoning God. Meditation is God phoning me and me listening.

SELF-COACHING QUESTIONS

- How are my challenges keeping me from fully enjoying life?
- How do I feel, really feel, about these challenges being in my life?
- Which challenge will I pay attention to first?
- What keeps me from taking action to address this challenge?
- In what ways will my life improve when I work through this challenge?
- How is this challenge nudging me to grow personally?

Lesson 2: Own your life by taking responsibility.

The only thing we can control is ourselves. We can't control people, places, or things. Cleaning up our lives starts with owning them. We have the power of choice. It's easy to blame others. It's harder to take personal responsibility for our own lives. Be honest with yourself. It all starts with you.

Ways to increase personal responsibility:

Own your choices. Ask yourself:
"What part of this circumstance was initiated by me?"

Own your life.

- Identify the areas in your life for which you need to be responsible.
- Focus on **self** and resist the urge to look outside of yourself or blame others.
- List the ways you are hurting yourself and others by not owning your part.
- Stop complaining. Often we complain and project our feelings to a friend, a co-worker, or a family member as a way of taking the attention off of ourselves.
- Write out how you want the situation to look by bringing it to present tense.

SELF-COACHING QUESTIONS

- Who do I blame for what's going on in my life?
- To what extent am I responsible for what's happening?
- What feelings do I notice when I give voice to my inner complaints?
- What ideas do I have to make my situation better?
- In what ways will I feel better about myself when I start owning my life?

Lesson 3: Ask for help.

We are not made to be alone. No one is an island. We are made to be in relationships. We need the perspective, strength, and support of others in order to grow. Asking for help is a strength. Period.

Ways to ask for help:

Recognize that we're not our best when we do everything alone. *Sometimes we tell ourselves that it's right to rely fully on our inner strength. Yet, we are made to live our lives with other people. There are people in your life who can help you move in the direction of your goal, and will feel honored to provide help and feedback.*

Pray for clarity, wisdom, guidance, and peace on your journey. *My greatest source of strength is my faith in God. What is your source of strength? In what ways do you make a connection with God and reach for strength beyond yourself?*

Ask and you shall receive. (Matthew 21:22) *Getting help starts with asking for help. This Biblical promise is clear. A spiritual connection to God provides power beyond your own.*

Delegate. *Delegating at home or in the workplace fosters stronger connections, deepens relationships, and empowers others. It also promotes a sense of team. By trying to do it all, you will have less quality in your life and well-being. You are also taking growth opportunities from those you want to empower.*

SELF-COACHING QUESTIONS

- Who do I know who has faced similar challenges?
- What keeps me from reaching out to these people?
- How will I feel when I am getting the help I need?
- Pray the serenity prayer:

God, grant me the serenity to accept the things I cannot change, the courage to change the things I can, and the wisdom to know the difference.

Lesson 4: Practice.

I have always believed there are no failures or mistakes, only experiences. Experience is our best teacher. We get to practice. Keep practicing because it is through repetition that greatness is developed. Practicing develops stamina, character, and determination to do a little bit better. Over time, what you practice saying or doing becomes second nature. It becomes *you*.

Ways to develop the skill of practice:

Consider the small steps that lead to large improvements.
If you were learning to play the violin, you would quickly realize that improvement only happens through practice. It's unlikely that you would be able to master the art of your violin in a few hours. Self-improvement is the same: It is a series of small steps. What improvements are you working toward? What steps can you practice moving in the direction of improvement? Which step will you practice first?

Strive to be patient with yourself.
Improvement takes time. Be realistic with yourself about what your self-improvement journey will look like. Congratulate yourself for the small steps you take each day. You're getting better, one step at a time.

You can make a change quickly, but lasting change takes time, repetition, and practice.

SELF-COACHING QUESTIONS

- What small steps can I take to lead to the large improvements I'm looking for?
- What can I let go of to make more time for practicing?
- What keeps me from being patient with myself?
- What benefits will I receive by committing to consistent practice?
- What feelings do I have when I choose to practice a skill repeatedly?
- Is what I am practicing moving me closer to my goal, or further away?

Lesson 5: Choose between the pain of discipline or the pain of regret.

None of us wants to live in regret. The pain of discipline leads us to feel stronger as we live lives with more intention and purpose. Regret can't be changed because it is in the past. You can choose to release its hold on you. It can be released.

Ways to choose:

Consider the pros and cons of change.
Think about self-improvement as a significant choice in your life. On one side of a sheet of paper write down the benefits of improving what you want to improve. On the other side jot down what could be painful about change. How will discipline move you toward your goals?

Create a ***flip the switch*** moment.
Go from the pain of regret to the pain of discipline.

- *The pain of regret tears down esteem and confidence.*
- *The pain of discipline builds up strength and personal power.*

Let go.
Ask God to help you let go of past regrets and empower you to make new choices.

SELF-COACHING QUESTIONS

- What is living in regret costing me?
- What is holding me back from choosing the pain of discipline?
- How will I release any regret that is keeping me from all I am created to be?
- Where do I need to strengthen my self-discipline?
- How will I remind myself of what is important along the way?

Lesson 6: Focus on what you want to create in your life.

What we focus on expands or gets bigger. Until you become fully aware of what you want to create in your life, you might have moments where you wonder, "Why does this keep happening?" In some cases, you might be inclined to just give in to the fact that life is "just this way."

You get exactly what you focus on. When you stay focused in your thoughts about a problem, it simply gets bigger. It's likely that you will attract more of the same situation in your life. By being a deliberate thinker, you empower yourself to make shifts and changes. This is where practice comes in. We have to practice in order to get better and need to allow ourselves grace along the way.

Consider journaling.
Many people benefit from journaling, a simple practice where you chat with yourself through writing. Through journaling, you can capture thoughts and feelings about what's happening in your life. Journaling helps you write the story of what you want your future to look like.

Identify what you want to shift or change.

Set an appointment daily or weekly to practice.

Measure results and celebrate you.

SELF-COACHING QUESTIONS

- What do I want more of in my life?
- What would a perfect day look like?
- How does my "perfect day" compare to the days I am living now?
- What, specifically, means the most to me?
- What will it take to bring that to life, here and now?

Accept your life's invitations to grow. Cleaning up my life resulted in amazing transformations that changed the course of my life significantly. What changes might be on the horizon for you?

Even on days that are dark and cloudy, the sun is shining. It's there, shining behind the clouds. Sometimes you can see tiny beams of light breaking through the clouds, reminding you that the sun is always shining. Some days you just can't see the light. Keep the faith. Faith means believing before seeing. Know that the light is there, ready to shine brightly on you.

Flip the switch from darkness to light. Become more aware. Own it. Ask for help. Practice. Make choices so you can create a life you love.

> *We must all suffer from one of two pains:*
> *the pain of discipline or the pain of regret.*
> *The difference is discipline weighs ounces,*
> *while regret weighs tons.*
>
> - JIM ROHN

MY THOUGHTS
AND REFLECTIONS

―――∞♡∞―――

....
....
....
....
....
....
....
....
....
....
....
....
....
....
....
....

CLEAN IT UP, ONE THING AT A TIME

MY THOUGHTS
AND REFLECTIONS

‌

‌

‌

‌

‌

‌

‌

‌

‌

‌

‌

‌

‌

‌

‌

CLEAN IT UP, ONE THING AT A TIME

CHAPTER TWO

MIND YOUR MINDSET

When you change the way you
look at things, the things you
look at change.

- ESTHER HICKS

CHAPTER TWO

MIND YOUR MINDSET

It was a warm sunny evening in Seattle, and I was visiting family and friends for a long weekend. As the sun began to set behind the majestic Olympic Mountains, my mom yelled, "Joan, hurry! The sun is going down! You don't want to miss this! It's going to be the best one ever!" The urgency in her voice would have made you think it was solar eclipse, something you only see once every few years.

I raced out of the kitchen, my socks sliding on the hardwood floor. In that moment I felt like I was about to miss the best part of a movie. I chose a mindset of excitement and optimism, and it made watching the sunset feel like a once-in-a-lifetime experience.

The Puget Sound is known for its beautiful sunsets. They're breathtaking. I don't know if my favorite part was watching the sunset or hearing the excitement in my mom's voice as we watched the sun vanish into the Pacific Ocean. She would say with a wink, "They don't see this in Kansas." Followed by, "What did you think? Best one ever?" We would laugh and look at each other with a grin.

Whether a sunset was or wasn't the best one ever, we would claim it was. It was what we believed it to be. It was a choice to see each sunset as the best one ever. That was our mindset.

In this chapter we will unpack how your thoughts and beliefs establish your mindset. As you become more aware of your mindset, you will see that making intentional choices to live a life you love starts with the mindset of believing such a life is possible for you. I will share simple mindset tools that have changed the quality of my well-being and daily living. As you check in with yourself and practice these tools, you will find what once had you stuck will be something you can confidently overcome.

We can choose the way we look at a situation. For me, *flipping the switch* has become a fun game that empowers me to live more deliberately by my choices. My positive mindset pays big dividends in the quality of my relationships. I invite you to open your heart and mind as you discover how claiming an empowering mindset will level up every area of your life.

> *The ultimate freedom we have as human beings is the power to select what we will let our minds dwell upon.*
>
> – DALLAS WILLARD

What is mindset?

A mindset is a set of beliefs that influences the way you look at yourself and the world around you. Beliefs can empower you and form a mindset that elevates you and lights you up. Or beliefs can create a limiting mindset that keeps you in the dark. We are all influenced and controlled by our beliefs. What we believe and think about become reinforced.

Beliefs often begin to develop in early childhood from our family, what we were taught in school or at work, the news, and our own experiences. With awareness, beliefs can be changed at any time. Change in a belief can be *flipped* based on awareness, new information, or when a person is ready to make a change. On the other hand, some beliefs are so powerful we never question them throughout our lifetime.

Reframing for a positive mindset shift

We can't control outside influences; however, we can control how we choose to look at them (just like the way my mom and I chose to see the sunset). I make feeling good a priority. When you choose to see and recognize the good in your life, you will begin to feel better immediately. Feeling better will elevate your mood and enhance the quality of your life.

We're all made up of energy, and the energy we give off is our vibration. Let's look at examples of simple ways to reframe common word choices that have low vibration. Reframing changes the way we look at circumstances. Reframing forces an intentional mindset shift. Practice reframing and watch the quality of your mindset, your day, and your life elevate. It's nothing but blue skies for you!

Flip the switch! **... from low vibration statement**	**... to elevated vibration statement**
Disempowering statements	*Empowering* statements.
I am so busy.	I am blessed with an abundant life.
I can't do that.	I give my best effort to succeed.
It is what it is.	It will be what I make it, and it's going to be great.
I am so tired.	It feels good to accomplish my daily tasks.
I failed again.	I commit to practicing and learning more every day.
I never get it right.	With practice, I discover more of what I want and don't want.

Have you ever heard yourself say "low vibration" phrases? They take their toll on your energy and your mindset. Reframe your thoughts. Create positive energy by choosing to develop a bright mindset.

How do you view failure and challenge?

Another place where reframing can change the way you look at something is in the way you think about failure. The word "failure" feels demeaning to me. I prefer a mindset that allows me to see a "miss" as experience. I have learned to ask myself, "What am I learning?" This question invites me to choose another perspective and look at challenges as opportunities to strengthen myself. I think of what those uncomfortable feelings are teaching me. I think of what I am learning. I keep practicing. I think of how overcoming my challenges increases the value I can bring to others.

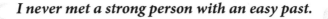

I never met a strong person with an easy past.

-TRACEY VLAHOS

Life isn't always easy. There are times when we find ourselves at a fork in the road, where we can choose either to shut down or rise up and embrace the challenges in front of us. I encourage you to be in touch with yourself. Pay attention. Ask quality questions and ask for help. Be open so you can get to the root of what is going on inside of you. Be willing to shift your mindset by reframing what you see.

Practice reinforces habits.

Each week I host multiple Morning Mindset Zoom meetings for team members who are committed to making ongoing positive mindset shifts. These sessions give team members a place to talk about what's happening in their lives and businesses, and explore how they can reframe their thinking to create more positive results. The tools that I am going to share with you throughout this chapter are tools that I teach weekly in the Morning Mindset sessions.

I recently asked a regular attendee to share what it was about the Morning Mindset calls that has kept her coming back twice a week for the past two years. She shared three reasons:

By intentionally focusing on her mindset, she ...

1. Powerfully kicks off her day to a successful start.
2. Practices one new skill and builds on what she learns weekly.
3. Consistently challenges and strengthens her mindset and feels more empowered to help her team members.

It has been inspiring to witness her growth and transformation. Like the other participants, she has discovered how mindset makes a difference. She has learned to reframe situations to choose a more positive mindset. She has formed the habit of paying attention to her mindset.

To change and grow, my thoughts
must be bigger than my feelings.

– DAVID BYRD

What do you need to **start** doing?

What do you need to **stop** doing?

What do you need to **keep** doing?

Spark your thinking with a 21-Day Reframe Challenge.

The majority of our challenges have very little to do with knowing "how" to do something. The challenges are finding the *courage* to decide and practice and the *discipline* to **do** the work that will create lasting change. Let me nudge you to get started now, to spark new thinking. Are you ready to take the 21-Day Reframe Challenge?

1. Write five limiting belief statements.
2. Reframe the limiting beliefs to empowering "I AM" statements.
3. Write your new statements on colored sticky notes.
4. Stick the notes to your bathroom mirror where you see them daily. Your subconscious will benefit from the positivity and empowerment.
5. Say the new statements out loud to yourself in the mirror, morning and night, for 21 days.

Example:

Low Vibration statement (Disempowering):

I don't have enough money to do the things I love.

Reframed to Elevated Vibration statement (Empowering):

I am a person who easily and effortlessly makes money to do all the things I love!

This exercise will help you become more aware of your mindset. You will begin to see things differently. You will find that you're able to *flip the switch* more swiftly. You will discover that it's easier to get unstuck when you choose an empowering mindset.

There are people who naturally look for the good in every circumstance. The silver lining is always there if we look for it. There are also people that choose negative or fear-based thoughts. They often live in those patterns and wonder why their conditions don't improve. Nothing improves if WE don't improve.

> *I am not what has happened to me.*
> *I am what I choose to become!*
>
> - CARL JUNG

There have been times when I stayed stuck for much longer than I care to admit. When I need to coax myself through a struggle, I pause, close my eyes, and imagine how I will feel *after I take action*. I like to say, "Play the tape through." This fuels me to do what sometimes I don't want to do. I focus on the *feeling of accomplishing* the task, goal, or dream. When I consciously attach the feel-good emotions to accomplishing the task, it gets me going in the right direction.

As we explored in Chapter One, journaling will increase your awareness of thoughts and feelings. In the midst of a challenge, journaling will help you think through what is happening in your life. Putting your thoughts and feelings in writing can help you redirect your energy and guide you to a new route that is more positive.

Mindset for manifesting

The heart opens to the thought. The brain thinks and feels the experience. Bringing the thoughts and feelings to pen and paper is the beginning step to manifesting anything you desire.

I remember when the experience of building a home reinforced my learning and mindset for manifesting belief. Our house plans were finished, and it was time to break ground. My husband and I were excited to see our new home come to life. We hadn't decided on our colors or details. You may have heard the phrase, "What you think about you bring about." I decided it was time to think about what I wanted my home's interior and exterior to look like.

I had recently trained my team on the impact of dream/vision boards. Creating a vision board involves making a collage of images, photographs, and affirmations of your dreams and desires that inspire and motivate you to take action. I created a board about our new home. Browsing through magazines, I looked for photographs that captured the feeling I wanted to create and images that reflected my desired style. I tore out photographs of every detail: window trim, kitchen counters, paint colors, fixtures, and furniture. I glued the pictures to my board. I wanted to look at my board each day, so I leaned it against the wall on a tall dresser.

I remember my feelings as I looked at the pictures. I could feel my family all together living in that home. I could envision us playing board games and eating at the dining room table. I could almost smell the food cooking on my state-of-the-art kitchen appliances. My home would be a place where family and friends would gather. It would be a home where kids wanted to swim in the pool, laugh, and have fun. Creating the images of life in our new home made the two-year construction process seem shorter.

One day my vision board quietly slipped behind the dresser. I didn't even notice it was gone. When moving day arrived, I pulled the tall wood dresser from the wall and my "Dream House" vision board appeared. I began to cry tears of joy as I dusted off the pictures. My new home was now done! I was blown away to see that while the vision board never came with me as I shopped for every finish, the images perfectly reflected the style and feel of my new home. They were etched in my mind and were now a reality.

What we think about and believe becomes reinforced. When I browsed the pages of the magazines, I thought about what I wanted. As I pasted each image on my board, I believed each detail could happen. What we think about, we bring about. This is how manifesting works.

Die with memories, not with dreams.

- ROB SPERRY

Create your own morning ritual.

Mindset isn't something I learned in school. I have developed a positive mindset through practice. Something that has made a difference to me is establishing a morning ritual. This is a consistent practice that significantly influences the quality of each day.

I used to figure out the least amount of time it would take me to get ready and sleep right up to moment the alarm would ring. Sometimes I would even hit the "snooze" button a few times. I would wake up feeling rushed, uneasy, and stressed.

Once I had a family, I became more aware of the importance of self-care. I needed to take good care of me so I could take good care of them. I became more disciplined with my time, choosing to get up a little earlier to enjoy some quiet time. I liked the idea of time where no kids would need me and no phones would ring. Peaceful moments with my morning coffee became essential to starting my days right. My morning ritual would start with prayer. This would set my mindset for an incredible day. Some days my morning ritual would take less than five minutes. It's amazing what this little extra time did for the quality of my days.

Joan's Morning Mindset

Today, my morning ritual remains an essential part of each day. I call this my "Mindful Morning" time. Here's what my ritual looks like:

- **Stillness.** I pause for a few moments of stillness so I can become aware. I take a few minutes after the alarm to focus on my breathing. I take a few slow deep breaths from my belly, breathing in through my nose, and releasing through my mouth.

- **Gratitude.** I thank God for the day.

- **Prayer.** I ask God to direct my thinking and turn my will and life over to Him. I ask for guidance: "Show me who to help today."

- **Meditation.** I take a few minutes to breathe and meditate on the way I want the day to unfold.

- **Daily Planning.** I get up, turn on music that awakens my soul, and grab my cup of coffee. I sit in a peaceful place and visit my planner, and check emails and messages.

It will take intentional effort to establish your own morning ritual. Often it can take several attempts to form a new habit. If you need a break, stop or restart the next day. Be gentle with yourself. Give yourself grace. Don't give up on yourself. Remind yourself that you are learning a new habit and you are practicing. Talk positively to yourself. Practice makes permanent. As you create your own morning ritual, pay attention to how you feel. Notice how the quality of your day improves.

Talk to yourself with kindness.

Like all of us, I have conversations with myself throughout the day. If I am not careful and selective about my thoughts, I can easily fall into a rabbit hole. Have you ever noticed we often talk to others with more grace and kindness than we do when we're talking to ourselves? If you ever hear an inner dialogue that's beating yourself up for what you **should** have done or you're thinking about what you **need to** do, or **have to** do, pause. Take a deep breath. Let go of judgment. Remind yourself to talk to yourself with kindness and grace, the way you would chat with a friend.

Your relationship with yourself is the most important one you'll have. It determines the quality of your relationship with others, and it helps you connect deeply to what is most important to you. What is the tone of the conversations you have with yourself?

Instead of this ...	*Flip the switch ...*
I should ...	I will **choose** ...
I need to ...	I **want** to ...
I have to ...	I **get** to ...

Let go of self-judgement. Take charge of the thoughts you allow into conversations with yourself.

HALT! Sometimes, we need to stop to refuel ourselves!

Your mindset evolves as your day unfolds. It helps to periodically ask yourself questions to understand why you are feeling the way you are. Sometimes you can pause to think about the "why" behind your feelings. It is easy to stay in our misery, stuck in self. I'd like to share an acronym that helps me check in with myself and take action to quickly change my state of mind when I need to.

HALT = Hungry. Angry. Lonely. Tired.

If you feel yourself spiraling into a funk, ask yourself these questions:

- What has me feeling this way?
- Am I hungry, angry, lonely or tired?
- What do I need to do to get out of this funk?

It feels much better to DO something to get out of it. Here are a few ideas to change your state of mind:

1. **Play upbeat music.** It's easy to reach for your phone to power up some of your favorite tunes. You'll immediately change your mood.

2. **Eat foods that fuel you.** Choose protein, a salad, nuts, or fresh berries. To avoid crashing, avoid high-sugar foods.

3. **Move your body.** Take a walk or an exercise break. It will energize you.

4. **Breathe.** Oxygen is energy. Pay attention to the way you are breathing. (You'll learn more about breathing techniques in Chapter Four.)

5. **Help someone else.** It may help to step away from your current environment and connect with another human being.

6. **Rest.** Sometimes no matter what time it is, it is time to turn OFF. Honor your mind and body! Give them the rest they are calling for.

The easiest way to stop a feeling from gaining momentum is to do something completely different. Resistance comes when we try and stop thinking and feeling a certain way. My dear friend, Star, says, "Thank the feeling for what it is showing you." Think differently. You will find that you can easily *flip the switch* by redirecting yourself with high vibration activities.

Balance logic with emotion.

Sometimes when emotions are high, logic is low.

- SHANNON SHARPE

When I am in a challenging situation, I have learned to listen more and act less. We process information with both emotion and logic, yet in the midst of an emotionally charged situation, it can be a struggle to think clearly. I often "sleep on it" and allow the emotion and logic to come into balance.

It may seem like a lot of work to make daily choices that foster a positive mindset. I can assure you that the quality of your life is dependent on your mindset. It isn't easy to make shifts and changes and practice new skills. The self-confidence gains you will experience will draw out more of your true nature. Who you are created to be will take the right of way and shine through you like never before.

Sometimes you just have to start all over differently.

- BERNARD KELVIN CLIVE

Recognize when it's time for a Total Mindset Reboot.

There are times in life when something unexpected happens and a detour is the only way through it. You are familiar with the concept of a highway detour, right? Detours force us to find new routes to reach our desired destinations. They rarely come along at convenient times. When a detour presents itself, whether on the highway or in your life, an entire mindset reboot is often necessary.

For a moment, picture this driving scene in your mind:

- You're traveling to a fun location for a friend's beach wedding.
- You are following the directions, even though they aren't familiar.
- You remain committed to getting to the wedding.
- On your journey, you picture the happy couple, feet in the sand, sun shining on their special day.

Out of nowhere, you see a sign that says, "Detour."

- You need to find a new route.
- You instantly feel uncomfortable.
- A few choice words may slip out of your mouth.

Now, you don't stop and turn back because of this unforeseen circumstance. You want to go to the wedding, so you dig deeper. You are determined! You fire up your GPS to create a new plan. You remind yourself that you can't control this.

This driving scene is not really any different from bumps in the road in your life or business that call for a total mindset reboot. The circumstances can strengthen you. Many give up at the first sign of a struggle because of the way they choose to look at the situation. Even a baby chick must peck its way into this world. It is process. The process of leaving the egg is what strengthens it to survive.

How could you do an immediate Total Mindset Reboot on your way to that wedding? Let's take a look:

- I am thankful we aren't caught in the traffic back-up.
- I am glad we left early with plenty of time to spare.
- I am thankful there is another way to get there.
- I am still excited and look forward to celebrating with our friends!

Can you see how this Total Mindset Reboot had you embrace the new route and continue the journey with a spirit of positivity? Others might complain the whole way. Who would you rather ride with in the car? Need I say more?

Your mindset has everything to do with how you view any situation and how you choose to see the world. More importantly, mindset affects your relationships. Mindset starts with your relationship with yourself. Think of strengthening your mindset the way you think of building muscles at the gym. As you practice developing your mindset, be good to yourself. It takes time, commitment, and practice. Each step you take will build endurance, and endurance is what will separate you from the pack.

> *A year from now you may wish*
> *you had started today.*
>
> - KAREN LAMB

It's simple to work on your mindset. Find the determination to stick it out even when things get tough. Become the best version of yourself by cultivating a mindset that is positive and bright. The little moments you invest in yourself will add up. You will be glad you did the work.

Do you want to create the habit of
saying positive affirmations?
Download today:

Joan's Favorite Affirmations to
flip the switch:

www.joanrobison.com/JoansFavorite
AffirmationstoFlipTheSwitch

SELF-COACHING QUESTIONS

Take time to assess your mindset. Be honest with yourself.

- What is one area where choosing a new mindset will improve the quality of your life?

- By nature, are you pessimistic or optimistic?

- What can you do to choose a new perspective so that struggling through a challenge feels better?

- What will a daily ritual do to elevate your well-being for the day?

- How will developing a stronger, kinder, and more graceful relationship with yourself improve your relationship with others?

TAKE ACTION NOW!

It's time to get moving and put to work what you have learned.

- Choose one area of your life for which you will develop and practice a new mindset.

- Schedule a 15-minute appointment with yourself once a week to evaluate your progress.

- Make a list of activities that will raise your vibration and pull you out of a funk.
  Examples:
  - ✓ A walk
  - ✓ Music
  - ✓ Breathing
  - ✓ Reading affirmations

Remember: What you are drawn to and makes you feel better raises your energy vibration.

MY THOUGHTS
AND REFLECTIONS

MIND YOUR MINDSET

MY THOUGHTS
AND REFLECTIONS

MIND YOUR MINDSET

CHAPTER THREE

OVERCOME
YOUR FEARS

*Everything you want
is on the other side of fear.*

- JACK CANFIELD

OVERCOME YOUR FEARS

You know the feeling. Your heart beats a little faster. Your palms may get a little sweaty. Your stomach might act up. Your body could be telling you something. Your physical symptoms may be signs that you're in fear.

When I use the phrase "in fear," I'm referring to a state of the heart that keeps you from moving forward. Most people don't run toward fear. Instead, they convince themselves that staying away from fear will keep them comfortable. Unintentionally, they choose to live in fear.

I can easily recognize when my emotions, physical self, and spirit are off. Can you? When I notice that I'm out of alignment, the first thing I sense is that I'm not at peace. I ask myself, "What's really going on with me? Why am I feeling this way? What am I afraid of?" Most often I can see signs of fear. My head tells me to pay attention. My heart tells me to choose love instead of fear.

> *Deep down, at our cores, there are*
> *only two emotions: love and fear.*
> *All positive emotions come from love,*
> *all negative emotions from fear.*
> *From love flows happiness,*
> *contentment, peace, and joy.*
> *From fear comes anger, hate,*
> *anxiety and guilt.*
>
> -ELISABETH KUBLER ROSS

Most of us want more happiness, contentment, peace, and joy in our lives! So, let's work on overcoming fear. In this chapter we will explore several types of fear and how to work with each of them. We'll look at common fears and consider questions that can challenge your thinking. You will discover five tools that can help you get you out of fear more quickly, tools that can help you *flip the switch*.

As you read this chapter, I encourage to you to underline everything that speaks to you. I encourage you to work on becoming more aware of fears that get in your way. You can overcome your fears and become more of who you are created to be. Recognize that fear only has the power you choose to give it.

Are there times we need help to deal with our fears?

Sometimes fear is so extreme that it is best to address it with a professional therapist or coach. Had I not talked through my fears with a trained professional, those fears would have repeatedly shown up in my life. Fear rarely goes away on its own. I encourage you to get the help you need when you need it. Often, your primary care physician can refer you to a skilled professional.

Is all fear the same?

While the physical symptoms of fear are similar, our day-to-day fears may not be. Fear may be healthy, disguised, or known. Let's look at fears I've identified in my life; they may appear in your life, too.

Healthy fear

Sometimes a fear is completely justifiable. Healthy fear protects us from harm. For example, it is healthy to fear a fire, tidal wave, tornado, or countless other disasters. The feeling of fear inspires action. Think about the fear that overcomes you when you when you encounter danger. Maybe you unexpectedly come upon a frightening insect, snake or, worse yet, a wild animal when you're out for a walk. Maybe you hear a sound at your door when you are home alone. An immediate gut feeling will tell you that you need to take action. Fear can be healthy! It instinctively inspires us to respond by acting.

I lived in Mexico for a few years in the 1980s. During hurricane season, heavy rains would pound the city. Winds would kick up to such a high speed that they uprooted palm trees. Hurricanes were real and dangerous, and my head was filled with thoughts of destruction. I could feel my heart race and knew this was my body's way of sensing the clear and present danger. Neighbors with years of hurricane experience told me to stay inside. They showed me how to duct tape an "X" across my windows to keep them from shattering. My fear was justifiable, and it nudged me to take action.

> *Let fear be a counselor, and not a jailer.*
>
> - TONY ROBBINS

Disguised fear

Sometimes fear disguises itself and we don't realize that what we might be feeling is rooted in fear. I see disguised fear frequently in my coaching conversations. Fear can show up as control, procrastination, or excuses. Let's look at each of these.

Control

Fear may be present when we demonstrate an unhealthy need to direct an event or another person's behavior. You have probably experienced a time when someone assumed too much control over you. Or perhaps you remember a time when you couldn't let go of something and held control so tightly that you made the people around you uncomfortable. You may recall a time when you micromanaged every detail of an event with the aim of achieving a specific, perfect outcome. As you think about it, can you identify what you were afraid of?

When we assume too much control, we're often afraid of what we don't know. We can be afraid we might be wrong. We might be afraid someone doesn't know as much as we think we know. We could fear failure and be thinking about how that might feel. Control is fear in disguise.

I was working with a coaching client who wanted to improve the effectiveness of her team meetings. She had noticed a steady decline in meeting attendance and thought leading meant she needed to take control of the situation. She felt like she had to be the one to make everything right. She came to me looking for specific steps to make her meetings more engaging and motivating.

As we discussed her approach to team meetings, I saw that she was doing most of the meeting work herself from planning the details to presenting the training. When I heard, "If you want something done right, you've got to do it yourself, " I paused. I sensed that she wasn't comfortable asking others to get involved because she was afraid of the outcome. She was afraid that others couldn't do things right. For example, she was afraid that if she asked someone else to deliver a training message, they might miss the mark. Control! She believed she was the only one who could create a meeting that was engaging, inspiring, and motivating. Yet, by doing everything herself, she failed to involve others, the very action that makes meetings engaging, inspiring, and motivating.

We worked together to get to the heart of the situation, which was fear disguised as control. We talked about how giving team members an opportunity to shine in front of their peers could build confidence and foster team spirit and community. We worked on calming her fears as she relinquished control. Over time, her meeting attendance improved. People felt more involved and connected. She came to realize that her need to control the situation, rooted in fear of failure, was getting in her way.

STRATEGY for working through fear disguised as control:

First, breathe. When you're deep in control, you are typically wound so tight it's hard for anyone around you to play a role. Ask yourself what it really is that you are afraid of. Imagine a different outcome. Think about your situation as clearly as you can and identify areas where you can let go.

Procrastination

Most of us are familiar with the concept of procrastination. Perhaps you've said, "I'll get around to that later," more than you'd like. Research has shown a clear connection between fear and procrastination. The more anxious you feel about failing, the less likely you are to take steps to begin a task.

Sometimes I procrastinate when I don't know how to do something. When I was new to posting on social media, I felt insecure about my messaging. I would ask myself, "What do I want to say? Will my posts be good enough for people to want to read them?" That kind of thinking was fear that led to procrastination.

I know how to procrastinate, and I expect you do, too. I can find ANYTHING to distract me from doing something that I truly fear doing. For example, I might find myself cleaning out that drawer under the coffee pot that I've been meaning to get around to. Or I might convince myself that instead of working on my project I need to make a quick trip to the grocery store. Are these tasks essential? Most of the time they're not. I can convince myself of pretty much anything when I want to distract myself. Can you relate to this?

STRATEGY for working through fear disguised as procrastination:

When you catch yourself procrastinating, pause to reflect on what you're really avoiding. If you don't have enough physical energy right now to do what you need to do, schedule the task for a time when you'll be at peak energy. If you're feeling fine but still reaching for distractions to keep you from doing something, have an honest conversation with yourself. It might look like this:

- *Could fear be disguising itself as procrastination here?*
- *What is making me feel afraid?*
- *What could a positive outcome look like?*
- *How will it feel once I've accomplished this?*
- *What is my first step?*

It works well to set a timer and commit to working on your task, distraction-free, for 30 minutes. After that time, you can choose to keep going or stop. Often, the simple act of starting will reduce your fear and get you thinking in a new way.

Excuses

Excuses are often an attempt to let ourselves off the hook from doing something we're afraid to do. Do you ever hear excuses from your children or team members? They believe what they say.

An excuse is a sale that we make to ourselves.

-SUE RUSCH

As a leader in network marketing, it's my job to partner with team members and team leaders who want more from their businesses. Yet, they often get in their own way. They can sell themselves on a story that's really fear in disguise. I often hear these excuses:

Excuse	Potentially fear in disguise
I want to earn more but don't have the time to take on more business.	I'm afraid of failing.
I don't like the incentive destination so I'm not going to go on the trip.	I'm afraid to be away from my family for five days. I am afraid I won't make the requirements.
I don't want to get team members to share their goals with me.	I'm afraid they'll think I'm pushy.

STRATEGY for working through fear disguised as an excuse:

When you catch yourself making excuses, ask yourself what's really going on. It could be helpful to have a frank conversation with a friend or a coach. Ask that person to help you identify any fear that could be showing up as unintended excuses.

If you see a team member's explanation as more of an excuse, set up a time to talk it through. Without accusing them of making excuses, ask gentle questions that help them get to the heart of what they might be afraid of.

We've looked at healthy fear. We've looked at disguised fear. Now let's look at known fear.

Known fear

You may be aware of fears that arise during specific circumstances in your life. A known fear could be public speaking. Or perhaps you feel a fear of heights or flying. These types of fears may be like anchors that hold you back from experiences you want or opportunities to grow.

> *Being brave isn't the absence of fear.*
> *Being brave is having that fear but finding*
> *a way through it.*
>
> - BEAR GRYLLS

It rarely works to wait for a fear to go away before taking action. By acting, you lessen the hold fear will have on you. One small step will help you feel brave as you move toward bigger actions. For example, if you're afraid to speak to a large group, first speak to a small group. It's highly likely that you will survive the experience! Next, talk to a medium-sized group, then a larger group. Remember: If you allow your mind to continuously replay thoughts about your known fears, you'll get in the habit of negative self-talk. Instead, develop the habit of taking action in the presence of fear. When you're willing to confront your known fears, and act on them; you can overcome them.

Common fears and questions to challenge your thinking

Whether you are in sales or leadership, or are simply aiming to live a richer life, at some point you've experienced fear. Fear resides within us. It has a way of paralyzing us.

Let's look at some of the most common fears in life, sales, and leadership. Because it's not enough to know that we're afraid, I'll equip you with questions that can help you get to the heart of what you're feeling and help you work through fear on your life's journey.

Common fears that show up in life.

When it comes to living a life we love, replaying fear-based thoughts can rob our energy and erode our self-esteem. Surly you've heard, "We are our own worst enemy." I see this with people I work with, as well as myself. Have you ever experienced any of these?

- *I am afraid they don't like me.*
    - Is this a fact or a thought?
    - Can I really change another person's opinion?
    - What makes me think they don't like me?

- *I am afraid things won't turn out perfectly.*
    - What does perfect look like?
    - Who decides if something is perfect?
    - What is *seeking perfection* teaching me?

- *I am afraid of what will happen if I don't make the right decision.*
    - How will I know a decision is right?
    - Is there something about indecisiveness that works for me?
    - What will I miss by remaining indecisive?

- *I am afraid to make a commitment.*
    - What in my experience makes me afraid to be **all in**?
    - How does committing one day at a time feel?
    - Is there a neutral person who can help me work through this fear?

- *I am afraid of taking the risk, it's nice here in my comfort zone.*
    - What am I really risking?
    - Am I growing when I stay in my comfort zone?
    - How can I *flip the switch* to change my perception of risk?

Common fears that show up in sales.

When it comes to selling, most fears keep us focused too much on "self." We think less about our customers and their experiences and more about our own experience. We get stuck in our perceptions instead of thinking about how we can serve our customers by delivering what they need and want. Have you ever experienced any of the following:

- *I am afraid that my customer or prospect will say "no".*
  - How do I know what my customers' needs are if I don't ask?
  - How can I re-frame the way I look at hearing "no"?
  - What open ended questions can I ask so I don't hear "no"?

- *I am afraid they will think I am pushy.*
  - What part of the relationship can I strengthen to feel like I am a giver instead of a taker?
  - What part of my offer seems pushy?
  - What needs to change so I feel like I am adding value to my customers' lives?

- *I am afraid that this business could take over my life.*
  - What boundaries can I set for myself so this doesn't happen?
  - How do I feel about using a calendar to manage myself?
  - How would making a list of my daily and weekly priorities allow me to see how this business can work?

- *I am afraid my geographic area is saturated and I have run out of customers.*
  - What research have I done?
  - How many people do I know who love the product I sell?
  - Am I thinking broadly enough? Where else can I sell my products?

- *I am afraid I don't have the right words to text or call.*
  - What have I done to prepare my messages?
  - Which benefits will I share, and what will I do to convey my enthusiasm?
  - What words would inspire me enough to respond?

Common fears that show up in leadership

Fear often holds people back from choosing a leadership role. I often see *fear of failure* develop from a perceived lack of experience. I see *fear of not knowing what to do* when someone doesn't fully understand the leader's role. People who are new to leading others often demonstrate *fear of communicating expectations*. They are afraid to hold others accountable. Inexperienced leaders often misunderstand communication and see it as confrontation. These fears show up as a lack of confidence. It's common to feel fear when you're new to any role. By accepting the challenge of leading, leaders build confidence. Here are some common fears:

- *I am afraid I may not know how to handle a situation.*
    - What did I learn in the past by working through an unfamiliar circumstance?
    - Who could help me work through the discomfort of the unknown?
    - How much value will I add by supporting people through challenges and opportunities?

- *I am afraid I will fail as leader.*
    - Is it serving me to base my self-worth on my current leadership skills?
    - How will learning as I go develop my leadership skills?
    - If I feel the fear and lean in, what is the best thing that can happen?

- *I am afraid to come across as a boss.*
    - How many people could I impact positively by building a team?
    - How will setting clear expectations empower others to grow?

- *I am afraid of the responsibility of being a leader.*
    - When I explored the specific responsibilities, what scared me the most?

- Who have I led in the past and how did I feel?
- What do I want to learn to elevate my knowledge of my responsibilities?

- *I am afraid of being criticized or judged by others.*
  - How do I reframe criticism?
  - How can I remind myself that I am striving to be the best I can be?
  - How is fear robbing me of moving forward in my leadership development?

It is important to understand that fear is present in our lives. It's even more important to find ways to work through fear so we can move closer to what we want in life. Learn to recognize common fears and ask yourself the challenging questions that will help you work through them.

Five Tools to help you flip the switch

Let's look at tools that can help you *flip the switch* and get back on course in the presence of fear.

TOOL #1: Acknowledge and accept the fear.

Be aware that you are in fear. Acknowledge and accept your fear so you can overcome it. Pause, feel the fear, and let it pass.

> *We cannot change anything*
> *unless we accept it.*
>
> -CARL JUNG

TOOL #2: Thank the fear and send it back where it came from.

I am a fan of talking yourself through a problem to a solution. Once you've acknowledged and accepted a fear, you must be willing to look deeper as to why it showed up and what it is teaching you. Pause to breathe and visualize:

- Take a few deep cleansing breaths. Settle into your body.
- Breathe in, and visualize confidence, strengths, curiosity.
- As you breathe out, visualize worry, doubt, anxiousness leaving you.
- Say "Thank you!"

TOOL #3: Redirect your energy to something that makes you feel good.

There are many ways to redirect your energy. My way is to stop the momentum by doing something completely different.

Consider these options to redirect your energy:
- Do something else that makes you feel good.
- Move your body.
- Breathe in deeply through your nose and out through your mouth.
- Put on music and you'll immediately raise your vibration.
- Exercise.
- Help a friend.
- Make a gratitude list.

TOOL #4 Get out of "self."

Getting out of self means thinking about other human beings, what they need, and how we can serve them.

I recall a conversation with a business colleague who was afraid of public speaking. She told me how she would work herself into high anxiety in the weeks and days prior to a speaking assignment. She asked if I had ever felt this way and what I did to increase my confidence.

I told her that in my first few years of public speaking there were times I would get so worked up that I made myself sick. I went on to share exactly what I did to *flip the switch*. I stopped thinking about me and started thinking about the people that I could help with my message. "If I can help just one person," I would say to myself, "this discomfort will be worth it." When we reconnected sometime later, she shared how the simple *flip* of *the switch* I shared changed everything for her. She couldn't believe the differences she could see in her business and her life. She felt more confidence and less fear.

TOOL # 5 Ask for help.

When people are in fear, they tend to isolate. Their best thoughts hold them back from solutions. Sometimes they believe that asking for help is a sign of weakness. They surmise that they should be able to do this on their own. As a result, they often stay stuck.

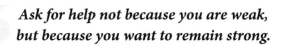

> *Ask for help not because you are weak,*
> *but because you want to remain strong.*
>
> - LES BROWN

Believe in yourself enough to know that getting help will make a difference. Your journey through fear may be smoother and swifter.

We have looked at types of fear and how to work with each of them. You're equipped with thoughtful questions that will challenge your thinking as you break through your fears. You have five tools to *flip the switch* and move yourself out of fear more quickly. Is it time to accept your fear and do what it takes to work through it?

Fear is a feeling. It's not right or wrong. It just *is*. You and I weren't designed to live lives of fear. We were designed to shine our light and live lives we love.

You gain strength, courage and confidence by
every experience in which you really stop to
look fear in the face.
You are able to say to yourself,
"I lived through this horror, I can take the
next thing that comes along."
The danger lies in refusing to face the fear,
in not daring to come to grips with it.
If you fail anywhere along the line,
it will take away your confidence.
You must make yourself succeed every time.
You must do the thing you think you
cannot do.

- ELEANOR ROOSEVELT.

SELF-COACHING QUESTIONS

Is it time to overcome your fears? Be honest with yourself.

- How is fear affecting my decisions on a daily, weekly, or monthly basis?

- If I feel fear creep in, what will be my chosen response?

- In my personal life or business, what fear constantly repeats itself?

- When I say, "I am fearless!" ... who do I see myself as?

TAKE ACTION NOW!

- What will you do now to overcome your fears?

- What is one fear that you will lean into this week?

- Using the tools you've learned, establish a new response to fear.

- Journal about the person you want to BE-come as a result of overcoming your fears.

MY THOUGHTS
AND REFLECTIONS

OVERCOME YOUR FEARS

MY THOUGHTS
AND REFLECTIONS

OVERCOME YOUR FEARS

CHAPTER FOUR

PRAYER, LOVE, AND MEDITATION

*Believe in God like you believe
in a sunrise. Not because you
can see it, but because you can
see all it touches.*

- C.S. LEWIS

CHAPTER FOUR

PRAYER, LOVE, AND MEDITATION

I knew that writing a book would be challenging. I knew it would take time. I expected that some chapters would be easier to write than others. What I didn't expect was that this chapter, the one most deeply connected to my heart and soul, would be the most difficult to write.

You may see the title of this chapter and immediately turn the page to see what comes next. Perhaps prayer and meditation are already a part of your life and what I share will affirm what you already know. You may find that the messages within this chapter validate what you are already doing to deepen your relationship with God. For those of you who have never prayed or meditated, you may awaken to an exciting new connection. Take what you want and leave the rest for someone else.

I'm not here to tell you what to believe, who to believe in, or what to call your God. One reason people stay away from experiencing God is that someone has told them what and how to believe. Often, people can't feel a person's caring spirit in conversations about faith and spirituality. They feel pushed. When we feel pushed, we naturally resist. It's like a child whose parent tries to control their every move. The child resists, feels unheard, unaccepted, and turns away and runs.

I'm at my best in the early morning. To get ready to take on a task, one way I set my mood is to create an environment that is filled with "feel good" elements. I put on the right background music to focus my energy. I light a candle. The morning I sat to write this chapter and share my thoughts and feelings about prayer, love, and meditation, fear crept in. I asked myself, "What if I offend someone?" I watered my plants. I folded some laundry. I cleaned my kitchen, which was already clean. As we learned in Chapter Three, fear is often disguised as procrastination and worry, keeping a person distracted and stuck in the dark.

I said to myself, "Enough of this, Joan!" I paused to practice what I preach. I took in a deep breath through my nose, and slowly exhaled through my mouth. I reminded myself that if I was to remain focused on these thoughts, I would be creating space for my ego to grow. I realized I needed to get out of my head and re-connect to God. I called back an acronym I once learned for EGO. I learned that ego prevails when we **e**dge **G**od **o**ut. I said a prayer and asked God, "How would you like me to share the greatest resource of all?" I closed my eyes and quieted my mind. I listened and waited. Thoughts of inadequacy began to quiet. As with most things God asks of me, when I take action, my work begins to flow.

In this chapter, I will share what prayer, love, and meditation mean to me and the impact they have made on my life. You'll learn how talking and listening to God provides direction much like a built-in compass. God is my greatest source of strength. I am confident in knowing God is present. God is good. God is love.

PRAYER

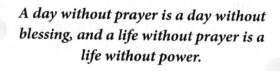

A day without prayer is a day without blessing, and a life without prayer is a life without power.

‐ EDWIN HARVEY

What is prayer?

Prayer is talking with God. Prayer can be asking for help or clarity. It can be elevating the needs of others. Or prayer can be a time of thanks for the blessings and abundance in your life. I think of prayer as talking to a best friend. It's easier than you think when you picture it this way. It doesn't matter where you are, what you are wearing, or even what you are saying. Prayer doesn't have to be rehearsed, long, or eloquent. Prayer is a time to connect with God. What matters to you matters to God.

I have noticed that confusion and fear can keep a person from building a spiritual connection with God. I often hear things like:

- "When I get my life together, I'll start to pray."
- "God doesn't like people like me."
- "When I have fewer problems, I'll go to God."
- "I am not spiritual enough."
- "Praying is a weakness."
- "I am afraid I'll have to change my life to be accepted by God."

These are examples of being stuck in the dark. There are no perfect people. Even the most enlightened person still has lessons to learn, or they wouldn't need to be here.

It can be uncomfortable and intimidating, even for the most confident person, to experience the physical building of a church or synagogue or their rituals. You can connect with God anywhere; these are simply the places where people gather. The church isn't the omnipresent God. The church is the people. Being part of a community, in fellowship with people, is important to growing spiritually. We are not made to go through life alone. We are not separate; we are all one.

> *Be still and know that I am God.*
>
> -PSALMS 46:10

In some situations, I don't know what or how to pray. Sometimes the answer is to be still and feel His presence as I hear Him say, " I am God." When I don't know where to begin to pray, one of the most powerful prayers I use is simple. I say, "Thank you," or "Help me," which acknowledges my need for Him. This expresses my gratitude and reminds me that He's got this. I feel burden after burden lift when I turn a problem over to God and leave it with Him.

By no means am I suggesting you do nothing to create a life you love. God provides guidance and leads you to take necessary steps. What matters to you matters to God. As you become more familiar with the true nature of God, you will begin to recognize His voice. You will intuitively know when to take action and when to stay still. The ways of God are simple.

Come as you are ... you won't leave the same!

At first, praying may not feel natural. It may feel awkward or even a little silly. You may have doubts, which is normal when learning something new. Know that your prayers can be silent, written in a journal, or said out loud. Start where you are most comfortable.

Think about learning how to ride a bike. I recall the apprehension I felt the first time my dad pushed me on my own. Riding a bike made me feel unstable. I wasn't certain if I trusted my skills or the bike. With practice I became more comfortable, and then the fun began. I bet you wouldn't think twice today about getting on a bike and pedaling down the road. Yet, when you first started, you felt like a fish out of water. The point is, sincerely try prayer before you decide it isn't for you. Ask God to reveal Himself to you in a way you will understand. He is sure to answer.

My prayer life deepened as my relationship with God evolved. At night my mom would do bedtime prayers with my brother and me. As I got older, I began to thank God and ask for help in a relationship way. The more I saw God work in my life, the more I was able to confidently trust. The rest was faith. I learned to let go of self-reliance and *flip the switch* to trust God. This is easier to say than do. I understand.

I often repeat affirming statements out loud. I say to myself, "Things are always working out for me." Or "The big picture is perfect." My life unfolds in the right timing, God's divine timing. Asking God to direct my thinking and my life requires me to surrender and trust. I feel less stress, have more relief, and am able to let go of the worries of the day. The most difficult circumstances of my life were not navigated by my human strength. They were navigated by walking in the light of the Spirit. I know that at times in my life, I have been carried.

The desires of your heart were placed there by God.

For more than ten years, I was in a Bible study with an amazing group of women. Most of us were in our twenties with new marriages and young children. Each of us had challenges. At times, we fell apart together. I witnessed some of the most miraculous transformations as God put us back together. Dee, our leader, was seasoned in her walk with God and knew the Bible as if she wrote it herself. She claimed that dealing with this group of women over the years is what gave her bloody knees. I smile whenever I think about how much she loved all of us. Dee was a true servant leader. She had a way of drawing you in and loving you as you were.

Once one of the women asked a question. "What if the desires of my heart aren't what God has intended for me?" Dee always knew what to say. She raised her right brow with interest and quoted several scriptures from the Bible that revealed how God longs to give you the desires of your heart. That wasn't enough for me. I wanted to know how I could be certain. I asked, "What if He doesn't really know how much I want what my heart desires?" I chuckle when I think about those early years of my spiritual journey. I may have lacked a measure of faith. Just a little. I thought I knew what was best for me. Dee looked at me with her intense blue eyes, and after a long pause she winked as she made it simple, saying, "He designed you. He placed the desires in your heart. If the desires of your heart are of love, they are of Him. Don't ask me, ask Him about it." And that was that. She made the complicated simple.

Dee always encouraged us to ask God and pointed us back to the power of the almighty God. Not one person in her study felt judged or condemned. You could feel her love. Her advice was practical and stemmed from the Bible and her own experience. She shined so brightly that she made people want to be in her company. She claimed that it was the Holy Spirit working through her.

LOVE

*There is only one happiness in
this life, to love and be loved.*

-GEORGE SAND

Love yourself so you can love others.

Love starts with you. The way you see yourself shapes the way
you see others. A person is only capable of loving at the level they
love themselves. You can't give away what you don't have. That
would be like someone with no money trying to give someone a
loan. It isn't possible. We may experience peace, joy, and openness,
but we can only give what we possess from within.

One of the reasons I began the journey of working on myself
was I saw qualities in other women that I hadn't developed yet.
Has this ever been true for you? I wanted to love and be loved, the
way I had seen others love each other. However, I needed more
practice to love my partner that way. I was more guarded and at
times afraid to show my feelings with actions. I know that fear
was at play, and where there is fear, love can't exist. What if I was
rejected? What if he didn't feel the same way I did? I had many
things going on inside me that needed to heal. While I spent hours
with a therapist talking about all the things that were wrong with
my partner, I knew that I had to overcome my faults to become
the woman I wanted to be. I know today that the difficulties I had
in relationships were due to me being emotionally distant with
myself. I didn't know how to love myself. I was conditional with
myself. I would think, "If I could just be good enough." And these
thoughts and beliefs contributed to broken relationships.

I found myself praying, "God help me." It was at that point that my life began to shift. I needed to own my life. Often, I pray for clarity with what is going on inside me. With awareness comes choice. With choice I take the next right steps for me.

I want to share a practice I learned from a gifted therapist. She taught me the practice of finishing this sentence: "I love the part of me that …" At this moment, I encourage you to pause and finish that sentence. What is true for you? Often it easier to say, "I **don't** love the part of me that …" The therapist taught me to love that part of me, too. There is a way to love every part of you. I encourage you to practice this often. Like me, you will find that as you build a stronger relationship of loving yourself, your capacity to love others expands, too. We cannot love others until we truly love ourselves.

Love is the very essence of God.

There have been periods in my life when living separate from God was my comfort zone. I had always believed in God and was raised going to church. Living separate from God was about me operating in self-reliance, being self-centered rather than God-centered. It was about relying too much on my human strength. As I look back to my times of darkness, the days of being disconnected didn't work out very well for me. A dear friend once told me, "We step away from God; He never steps away from us." It is a great reminder when I get going with the busy-ness of a day.

As we have explored in other chapters, as human beings we have free will to make choices each day. We choose the way we see the world, ourselves, and others. Our view is dependent on the condition of our hearts. Most of us believe love is a feeling; I believe love is a choice. Feelings come and go, but love goes on forever.

Show love in your actions.

Love thy neighbor as thyself.

- MATTHEW 22:39

God is love. We are meant to show love to one another. Beyond the deep love we show to a partner, family member, or dear friend, we can show love to many people in our lives by choosing actions that show love. What are your favorite ways to show love to others? Showing love can be as simple as:

- Making a caring phone call.
- Saying a friendly "hello" to someone who appears lost.
- Sending a hand-written card.
- Choosing an unexpected act of kindness.
- Giving a hug.
- Bringing a meal when someone is ill.
- The gift of presence as you share the gift of your time.
- Praying for their needs or general well-being.
- Being there.

I have learned so much about the character of love by watching my lifelong friends, Steve and Sally. One warm summer evening I had the pleasure of enjoying a patio fire at their home. Steve and Sally have been together since they were twelve years old, and even after so many years together, they still put each other first. In a conversation about their marriage, Steve was the first to speak up. With enthusiasm and a great, big smile, he said, "I want to be the best I can be every day for my wife!" I remember the moment I heard those words, thinking about how I wanted that kind of marriage in my life.

I have watched Steve and Sally take care of each other as if their marriage is the most important thing in their lives. Their days are filled with small acts of kindness out of love, not obligation. Often, Sally lovingly makes a cup of tea for Steve. They thoughtfully anticipate each other's needs. They radiate love. They radiate God.

To touch a heart, we must first offer a hand.

How would your quality of life be different if you were to focus on loving someone as they are? I can tell you firsthand this is one of the greatest challenges in my own life. After all, if people would just behave the way I think they should, everything would be better, right? (I laughed, too!)

Loving someone as they are means making peace with who a person is and accepting them, unconditionally, without the intent to change them. Without thinking about ourselves or what we want in return for our love. Without judgment. Meeting them where they are. This is what I call a higher level of living. It isn't about the person you are loving; it is about your ability to give love without expecting anything in return. It is about opening your heart to another, regardless of what someone has done or who they are. Love has no expectation. I am still learning to love more deeply, doing my best to release old habits and behaviors. Today I know that fear-based thoughts don't serve me.

To give and not expect return, that
is what lies at the heart of love.

- OSCAR WILDE

If you are a leader, coach, or trainer, you are naturally in the habit of assessing skills you see in your team members. It is your job to look for ways to guide people in the direction of continuous improvement. You may unknowingly approach other relationships in your life with a "coach to improve" mindset. What if instead of bringing a leadership approach into the rest of your life you were to simply care about the people around you, showing love to them as they are in the present moment? This takes intention. This takes remembering that love is accepting people as they are.

If you are an employer, you are accustomed to telling your employees what to do. It is your job to see situations and immediately think of ways to create improvements. It's what you do. While it may not be your intention to approach other relationships in your life with a manager's mindset, directing others becomes a habit. Loving others is about accepting them without regard for the need to change. In your interactions with the people in your life, what if you were to focus less on what needs to change and more on the good of the person? Relationships grow stronger when we choose to accept our friends and family members for who they are.

I have worked on meeting people as they are. I choose to see the best in people, reminding myself of where I came from. This perspective softens my heart from judging how I think they need to be. Instead of focusing on changing others, I look inside. Most times it's ME who needs to change. I have come a long way, and still there is work to be done. Each day delivers new opportunities for me to grow into the person I am created to be. How about you?

MEDITATION

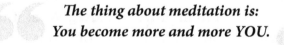

The thing about meditation is:
You become more and more YOU.

- DAVID LYNCH

What is meditation?

Throughout my day, I make time to meditate. Through meditation, I can quiet my mind and listen to God. When I started practicing meditation, my understanding was that I was to cease all thought. I kept trying this, but my mind was not able to turn off its thoughts. When I sheepishly asked a mentor about this, she laughed and said, "Unless you are asleep, you are thinking about something." What a relief! For her, meditation was a way to quiet the mind, slow thought, become aware, and be present in the now.

You might choose to listen to guided meditation, especially if you are new to meditating. Check online and you will find a multitude of options. Or you may simply listen to the rain or a sound in your home. I like to listen to the soothing sound of my water fountain as the water gently cascades. To me, meditation is spiritual medicine for my soul. It improves my body's overall well-being and my mind and spirit.

Benefits of Meditating:

- Reduces stress and anxiety.
- Helps with insomnia.
- Improves coping skills.

- Slows a person down.
- Increases focus.
- Raises a person's vibrational frequency.
- Increases conscious contact with God.
- Improves overall state of well-being.

When the challenges of a full day interfere with my daily meditation practice, I let it go. I don't beat myself up the way I used to. Instead, I offer myself the same grace I would extend to a friend who is doing her best. As I get back on track, my day improves. I am not an anxious person by nature, mainly because I am in constant motion. Meditation reminds me to slow down and listen to God within me. I crave this time and have come to need it like the air I breathe. Meditation keeps me in spiritual alignment and helps me maintain a conscious connection to God.

How, exactly, do I begin a meditation?

- Get into a quiet place. Sit up straight with feet flat on floor, and open hands on your thighs.
- Close your eyes and settle into your space.
- Become aware of your breathing.
- Start from the low belly. Slowly, draw a cleansing breath, inhaling through your nose, counting to 6-8.
- Fill your lungs. Allow the air to hover at the top of your lungs.
- Slowly exhale. Release all the breath through your mouth, counting to 6-8.
- Scan your body. Become aware.
  - How are you feeling?

- Is anything tight or painful?
- Visualize sending breath to any area that needs attention.

- As you turn your attention to the top of your head, begin to visualize drawing in a beautiful golden light.
- Take several breaths to fill your body.
- God is love. God is light. You are shining.

Meditation practices:

1. Focus on the repetitive moves of a ceiling fan or the hum of a nearby heater or air conditioner.
2. Choose a mantra, phrase, or an "I am" statement to repeat.
3. Check studios in your area to find yoga, sound therapy, and mediation classes.
4. Search online for a wide variety of guided meditations.

Meditation provides a way of learning how to let go. As we sit, the self we've been trying to construct and make into a nice, neat package continues to unravel.

- JOHN WELWOOD

Prayer is the spiritual connection between us and our chosen source of strength. Prayer allows us to acknowledge our humanness and ask for help. I rely on the power of God to work through me to carry out my purpose for being here.

Think about your spiritual life as it is today. How effectively is it working for you? As you think about the ways that prayer, love, and meditation fit into your life, open yourself to new possibilities. Consider the ways daily practices that include prayer and meditation improve all areas of your life.

I have heard it said that with age comes wisdom. I believe wisdom comes from God and usually happens with experiencing Him. Give prayer and meditation a try. For 21 days, aim to make this a new habit and journal your findings. If you have been living your life by relying only upon yourself, it might be time to *flip the switch*. God is in your corner. Feel the presence of God in your life and feel His love for you as you go about your days. The journey you are on isn't a destination, it is all about who you become along the way.

MY THOUGHTS
AND REFLECTIONS

PRAYER, LOVE, AND MEDITATION

MY THOUGHTS
AND REFLECTIONS

PRAYER, LOVE, AND MEDITATION

PART TWO

WORKING
WITH OTHERS

The best leaders create a vision,
and help others see possibilities
they may have never considered.

- JOAN ROBISON

HAVE A HEART FOR PEOPLE, THE SALE WILL FOLLOW

*Never believe that a few caring
people can't change the world.
For, indeed, that's all who ever have.*

\- MARGARET MEAD

CHAPTER FIVE

HAVE A HEART FOR PEOPLE, THE SALE WILL FOLLOW

I love helping people get what they want. Working in sales is fun for me! Helping someone win satisfies my soul. The selling process starts with our ability to connect with our customers and clients and build rapport. It requires getting out of self and focusing our attention on helping our prospects get what they need or want.

You might not know it, but if you love helping people, most likely you already love sales. In my experience, the most successful salespeople have a genuine heart for people. By opening their hearts and using their heads, they take the first step that leads to success: they uncover what's most important to their prospects. Effective sellers seem to do it effortlessly:

- They are sincerely interested in people.
- They focus on real conversations first, not the sales skill.
- They find common ground with their prospects.
- They offer genuine compliments.
- They ask open-ended questions to get to know people better.
- They listen to the prospect with 100% of their attention.

What you consider to be most important may be vastly different from what another person sees as most important. You don't have to agree with what others think and feel. To make a real connection, seek to understand people. The art of making a real connection lies in finding out what's most important to another person. (Pause.) Think about your favorite salesperson. What is it about her that keeps you going back to her? More than likely it isn't what she sells. It's how she makes you feel. You buy *her*.

> *You can have everything in life you want*
> *if you will just help enough other people*
> *get what they want.*
>
> - ZIG ZIGLAR

Establishing a connection with your prospects is an essential first step in the sales process. Some salespeople make the mistake of rushing this part of the sales process or skipping it all together. This is a huge miss. It's like wanting a delicious piece of cake and expecting it to just appear. You've got to bake the cake first, right? Instead of starting your sales process by focusing on the sale, begin by focusing on your prospect.

Experienced salespeople know that it often takes multiple contacts with a person before a sale happens. Significant purchases may take as many as 5-7 connections before a buyer feels ready to jump into a decision. It's important to remember that each person defines a "significant" purchase differently, so it helps to keep in mind that sales is a process. Each interaction, each step, builds that process. Your customer might not buy from you today, but when you make a memorable impression, there's a good chance they will buy when they are ready.

A person who initially buys from you is a customer. A person who repeatedly buys from you becomes your client. People buy from people they like, know, and trust, but first they have to like you. Let me ask you this: Are you likable? How would someone describe you?

> *Listen more than you talk. Nobody learned*
> *anything by hearing themselves speak.*
>
> -RICHARD BRANSON

Your customers draw closer when they feel you are genuinely interested in them.

Prospects can feel when the salesperson *isn't* interested in them. Next time you're with a salesperson, make it a point to notice clues:

- Ask yourself, "How am I feeling during this interaction?"
- Is the process following your agenda or the salesperson's agenda?
- Does the salesperson ask about your needs, or does she tell you about her amazing product or offer?
- In what ways does the salesperson show interest in you?
- When the interaction is over, think about the specifics of what would make you want or not want to return to them.

When I am on the buying side of a selling situation, I pay attention to how I feel. When I feel like it is all about the salesperson making a sale, I start to move away. In my mind I picture myself wanting to say, "I was planning to buy, but maybe not from you. I feel like you don't care about what's important to me." But what I usually say sounds more like, "I am just looking today, but I'll let you know if I need your help." We both lost right there. I didn't buy an item I wanted, and she didn't get a sale. Neither of us left the sales process feeling satisfied.

This can also happen when we are attempting to build connections online because we don't have a prospect's full attention. When I'm coaching salespeople, one of the most common challenges I hear is this: The salesperson doesn't know what to do when a prospect suddenly stops communicating with her. Most times, I only need to ask a few questions to discover the reason behind it. More often than not, our coaching discussion leads us to realize:

- The salesperson failed to make a heartfelt connection.
- The salesperson did not learn what was most important to the prospect.
- The salesperson skipped the "connection" steps altogether.

If this situation has ever happened to you, you are probably remembering past conversations. Ask yourself these questions:

- What did my first message to the prospect actually say?
- How did I show my prospect that I was more interested in her than in making the sale?
- When I revisit the prospect, how will I find common ground to connect?

Temperature Check

When I'm selling, I pay attention to body language, eye contact, and general well-being. I also pay close attention to every word my prospect says and how she says it. At the same time, I pay attention to my own words and how I'm saying them. When evaluating whether I am connecting with my prospects, I often ask myself these questions:

Are prospects:

- Moving closer to me?
- Moving away from me?
- Running for the hills?

If they are moving away or running for the hills, chances are I haven't connected with or shown enough interest in them. I tell myself to *flip the switch*. I purge any thoughts about making a sale. Instead, I refocus my energy and efforts on revisiting. It's never too late to make a connection.

Do what most salespeople aren't willing to do: revisit your prospect.

When you choose to make another contact with your prospect, you will be in the minority. When faced with what feels like rejection, most salespeople give up after just one or two contacts. Your mindset is essential to your success. Shift your thinking. Remind yourself that the sales process is all about your prospects and what is important to them.

Start your next conversation by talking about something that has nothing to do with your product or service. Be genuinely interested in your prospect's life. Find something you have in common or offer a compliment. It can also be helpful to offer a special discount or offer something for free. If you try this approach, the results just might blow you away.

> *To build a long-term, successful enterprise, when you don't close a sale, open a relationship.*
>
> - PATRICIA FRIPP

Is selling a new skill or something we've always been doing?

I believe we are all wired to sell. We sell all day long, usually without realizing it. We have been selling since we were small children. We started by selling to our moms by crying when we were hungry, needed a diaper change, or wanted a cookie. We learned that by expressing our **emotions** to our parents we could get what we wanted or needed. We were born to win at sales, and it started when we were babies.

We are often selling, even in our closest relationships, without even being aware of it. Let's say you ask your significant other where he or she wants to go to dinner. You probably think about what is important to you, such as the cuisine or the ambiance, and then you respond. Unknowingly, you are selling him or her on where you want to go. If you are like me, you might also consider the dish or the vibe that might be important to your partner at the restaurant you want. (Wink. Wink. This is *selling*.) You are clever. You're using selling skills to persuade your partner to choose a particular restaurant by showing what you both love at this restaurant. It really is that simple.

My First Lesson in Sales came from my Grandpa Carl.

I grew up in an entrepreneurial family in Poulsbo, Washington, a small Norwegian town. My grandparents owned two businesses in the heart of downtown Poulsbo. My Grandpa Carl and his brother, Joe, started a business in the early 1940s. These guys were fun and gregarious. They loved people and people loved them. I noticed that Grandpa Carl had friends wherever he went. I would ask him over and over to tell me his sales stories. I loved them. Grandpa Carl was a great storyteller with a unique ability to illustrate events with dramatic flair.

I remember a pivotal moment in my early childhood that set the stage for my future career in sales and leadership. Thinking I was grown up enough to start working (after all, I was in the fourth grade), I asked my mom if I could go to work at **The Brothers,** Grandpa Carl's store. I loved the store and spent many days after school observing the happenings there. My mom discussed this with my dad, and the next Saturday I was up early, gussied up, and ready to start my first day of work.

As my dad and I drove to the store, I could picture my grandma running the cash register and effortlessly tapping the keys without looking at them. My grandma, like my grandpa, was a friend to many. She was always kind to the customers, and people loved her. I admired how she smiled at the customers and wished them a great day while counting out their change. I guess you could say that selling was in my blood. I wanted to help people and make money.

My dad and I arrived at the store on that bright Saturday morning. My dad said, "Today, you are going to train with the Old Man," which was what he and his brothers called Grandpa Carl. My grandpa was tall, direct, and had a commanding way about him. He had a big personality. I was ready to be trained by Grandpa Carl. Instead, he looked down at me and smiled as he reached into his pocket, and pulled out a carefully rolled wad of cash. He put a twenty-dollar bill in my hand as he shared his secret to selling success:

> *Joan, the first thing you need to know about sales is that people need to like you.*
>
> - GRANDPA CARL

Every Saturday, my grandpa would put out a large, pink bakery box full of assorted donuts for his employees, friends, and customers. He told me to go to Sluys Bakery and get an assortment of donuts. I walked down the street, made my way into the bakery, and started picking out the donuts. I knew my grandpa liked maple bars, so I picked out a few of those. I was learning. People have to like you.

I can feel my grandpa smiling as I share my first lesson in sales with you. At such a young age, I learned how a sale really starts. This became important even before I started selling products. This lesson gave me the confidence as a teenager to connect with people who weren't in my immediate circle and to build more quality relationships. Grandpa Carl showed me how important it was to create connections and build rapport with people before trying to sell to them. His teaching was invaluable, and I use it to this day. Lesson learned: People have to like you first.

People will like you when you ...

- Smile more often and at more people. Your face is the first thing people notice about you. It makes you approachable and breaks any perceived barriers. Try it today at the grocery store.

- Ask them about what they love: their kids, their family, themselves. It indicates you are interested in their lives. People love to talk about themselves.
- Call people by name. We love it when someone remembers our name.
- Use the words "home" and "love" because they stir some of the most powerful human emotions.
- Give a few minutes of your time. It says, "I care."
- Write a personal follow up note. It may be considered "old school," but think how great you feel when you get a handwritten note in the mail.
- Make a personal phone call. It doesn't matter if they answer, but your effort speaks volumes. It shows you are thinking about them and that you care.

People often buy based on emotions, then justify their purchases with logic.

Why do we buy anything? Because we expect we will feel better having it than not having it. Sometimes, we see something we want and are overwhelmed with emotions. We tell ourselves that we've got to have it. Now. We often buy based on emotions and justify our purchases later with logic.

I recall a recent instance when I did just that: I made a purchase based on emotion. It didn't involve a salesperson, and the sales process happened in my own mind. Emotions were the deciding factor. Logic didn't come into play until the moment I walked out of the store.

On my way to a business trip, I walked past an airport gift shop. Out of the corner of my eye I spotted a small clip speaker I knew I would love for my trip. I enjoy a small speaker that has a powerful punch. I pictured myself in my hotel room, remembering that I love to play music when I am getting ready. It sets my mood. I like a high vibe feeling, and music changes my state almost instantly. I was excited to see that the speaker's Bluetooth would be easy to use. "Ooh, I can play my favorite playlist from my iPhone," I thought. When I saw that it was waterproof, I immediately pictured myself using it at the pool, beach, or even a bath! With emotions in high gear, I eagerly slid my credit card out of my purse.

Logic set in immediately after I exited the store. I began to play ping pong about buying the speaker.

PING:	That speaker cost more at the airport than I needed to spend for a speaker. Robbery!
PONG:	Do I really need this? No, I am going to be so busy on this trip that I might not have much time to use it.
PING:	Yes, I want it. This isn't a high-ticket item. I am not buying a couch.
PONG:	I want to listen to music in my hotel room. I love playing music while I get ready.
PING:	I am happy I bought it.

I could have saved a few bucks by ordering it online or going to Best Buy, but I wouldn't have had it for that trip. It was worth it to me to spend a few extra dollars so I could enjoy the music in my room. I was (and still am) happy with my purchase! As I stood in the gift shop, I could already picture the feeling I would have in my room.

Despite my inner ping pong conversation, I was able to quickly think it through. NO buyer's remorse. I circled back to my emotions about what was important to me and why I wanted it. The extra cost, which wasn't much, was worth having the speaker on my trip and beyond. People (including me) often buy emotionally and justify later with logic.

You will sell your product or service when you are sold yourself.

There are times when we have to re-ignite our excitement for what we are selling. Like a new car, selling is only new until we get used to it. When great salespeople lose their excitement, they find ways to re-ignite their passion and excitement for their product. The same is true if we don't believe in the benefits of what we are selling. We must find a way to strengthen our own belief. Or choose something we feel will benefit people.

Once you become familiar with what you're selling, you may notice that the excitement you initially felt for your products starts to fade. To strengthen belief and re-ignite your excitement, it helps to re-sell yourself. When this happens to you, look through your line of products and select 3-4 items that you haven't used for a while. Start using them again, paying attention to what makes them exceptional. For me, this might mean that I choose a new color of nail polish I haven't been wearing. Or I might use the skin care or try a new wellness product. Look at the products you sell and get excited about them all over again. Think about their true value. Think about the first time you used them and describe that feeling to a prospect.

Many years ago, a team member asked me to help her increase her sales. In one of our first coaching calls, I realized that we needed to work on the way she thought about what she was selling. We needed to increase her belief in the value of offering a skin care system. She explained to me that she had never used a product of such quality and at such a high price point. Nor had she ever used skin care in a system.

Our company offered a variety of individual products as well as a package that provided a total skin care system. I asked her a few questions about products she had used in the past and what she thought about the results of the product she was now selling. She told me she loved the feeling and overall result of her current product but had doubts as to whether her customers were going to pay the price for a total skin care system. What do you suppose her limiting belief was? The product? Or the price point?

Pretty obvious: it was her belief around the price point. She had never invested in quality skin care or a system at this price point. I asked what she felt would be a *reasonable* price, and followed with, "Wouldn't it be likely that we could only expect *reasonable* results from a product that had a *reasonable* price?"

I asked her about the women she knew. Did she know anyone who might want dramatic or exceptional results, as opposed to *reasonable* ones? Did she know anyone who might want anti-aging products? She thought about it and said, "Yes." Now we were getting somewhere. She was realizing that not everyone thought like she thought. In fact, others might have different needs and want different results. They might have other beliefs about how they value skin care. I knew she needed evidence to believe differently. I thought back to my days selling skin care at Estee Lauder.

I gave her a homework assignment to go to Nordstrom and watch the salespeople sell skincare. I told her not to stop at one counter, but to move around and watch several salespeople. Having worked there for many years, I knew what she would see. She would witness kindness. She would see salespeople who identified the needs of their customers. I was confident she'd see salespeople who truly cared about people. Salespeople who started with the best products, not because they were the most expensive but because they believed the best products offered the customers the most benefits, the highest quality, and the optimal results at the best price.

My team member excitedly reported back that she "got it." I love when this happens. The light went on. She was able to create a new belief based on her experience. She went on to be honored consistently as one of the company's top sellers. Guess which product she sold the most? Yup, the best skin care system we offered. She enthusiastically told everyone she met about our skin care systems. And she was using them! Not only did watching the Nordstrom's salespeople ignite her excitement, she also *flipped the switch* and developed a new belief about high quality skin care. She also had more fun, increased her sales, and made more money. Most importantly, she helped more people.

When you are completely sold on the value of your product or service, you'll be more confident when you're selling to others. Do something small every day to improve your beliefs and skills. Your sales skills can only get better when you do.

Avoid the habit of prejudging how people will spend their money.

Prejudging is a habit that separates us from selling success. We lose more connection, relationships and, ultimately, sales when we believe we know what the prospect needs, wants, or can afford. It's really none of our business how people choose to spend their money, so avoid deciding for others. We don't know what others value. Assume that everyone wants the best you have to offer. They will tell you if they don't.

I recall one Christmas while working at Nordstrom. An elderly gentleman came to my counter and asked for my assistance. At first glance, he appeared messy and unkempt. His clothes looked almost dirty. I came around the counter and asked, "What can I help you find?" He reached in his pocket and pulled out a list written on a paper coaster from a local restaurant. I was familiar with that restaurant and realized immediately that we had a common ground. We spent the next hour getting to know each other as we found gifts for his entire family. It turned out he was a fisherman in Alaska and hadn't been home for several months. He left Nordstrom that day with his list completed and arms full of wrapped gifts for everyone in his family.

For as long as I worked at Nordstrom, he came to shop a few times a year. I no longer sell products at Nordstrom, yet he still returns to me to buy other products for his wife, children, and now grandchildren. It's been over 20 years. He has become a lifetime customer and a lifetime friend.

Early in my career, I found myself in the habit of pre-judging. The energy I spent trying to figure out who would or wouldn't buy was exhausting. Not to mention, I was usually wrong. The first step to changing that habit was awareness. I learned that by expanding my belief and seeing all people as buyers, my world became bigger, and so did my earnings.

The gift of leading with the heart

Salespeople who lead with their hearts can significantly influence someone to feel special. The light shines through you and draws people to you. Showing interest in someone is the first step in connecting and building rapport. Kindness, compassion, and genuine interest are character qualities cultivated on the inside. Being interested in another person can be practiced, but it isn't a skill; it's a heart matter. It's who you are. Grandpa Carl had it right: people have to like you first, and the sale will follow.

I am convinced that most people buy because they believe they will feel better having the product or service they are buying. Tapping into their emotions first will not only create more connections and build more relationships but will also empower you to keep more customers for a lifetime.

Have a heart for people. The sale will follow.

- J O A N   R O B I S O N

Are you looking for simple ways to increase your sales?
Check out this easy download today!

Joan's Top Ten Sales Tips

www.joanrobison.com/JoansTop10InSales

SELF-COACHING QUESTIONS

Take time to challenge your awareness. Pause to evaluate your own beliefs and skills.

- **How will I strengthen my beliefs and skills about selling?**

  What you believe will make a difference in what you do.

- **How will you bring the lessons of this chapter to your life and business?**

  When in doubt, remember the story of Grandpa Carl: people have to like you first.

- **How can I improve in leading with my heart?**

  Leading with your heart is a gift, both to yourself and to those you serve.

- **How has this chapter inspired you to think about building relationships with people?**

  No two people are alike. Helping someone win helps cement your relationship.

TAKE ACTION NOW!

Time to move and put what you've learned to work.

- **To strengthen belief:**

  Visit a store. Interact with a salesperson, observe, and learn.

- **To elevate your selling skills:**

  Identify one area within your sales skill set that you will commit to improving over the next 30 days. Practice the activity. Don't be concerned with the result. Practice. Practice. Practice.

- **Build a customer/client list:**

  Schedule a time each day to make two new connections. Do it! By the end of the week, you will have made 10, and by the end of the month, you'll have made 40. How will that increase your momentum?

MY THOUGHTS
AND REFLECTIONS

....

....

....

....

....

....

....

....

....

....

....

....

....

....

....

....

HAVE A HEART FOR PEOPLE, THE SALE WILL FOLLOW

MY THOUGHTS
AND REFLECTIONS

HAVE A HEART FOR PEOPLE, THE SALE WILL FOLLOW

CHAPTER SIX

COMMUNICATE
CONSISTENTLY

*I see many young entrepreneurs struggle
with the fundamentals of growth in a
network marketing company. Their biggest
problem is leaning too heavily on the internet
and technology to build the business.*

- JORDAN ADLER

CHAPTER SIX

COMMUNICATE CONSISTENTLY

Communication skills are essential to living a life you love! Communicating adds depth to your life and effectiveness to your work. Effective communication increases the likelihood that you will be understood and that you will understand others. Communication will convey messages, thoughts, feelings, and points of view. Effective communication avoids misunderstandings that can lead to unnecessary conflicts. By practicing healthy communication skills, every area of your life will improve.

It wasn't that long ago that communication options were limited to face-to-face meetings, phone calls, or postal mail. Over the last two decades communication has become much speedier and easier. Email became commonplace, followed by text messaging, social media platforms, and even Zoom. While the ways we communicate change with the times, the need to actually connect has not. Just because a new way of communicating may appear simple or easy doesn't guarantee it is the most effective way to connect with customers, co-workers, or teams.

Warning! This chapter is very tactical, and it is filled with lots of lists and "how-to" suggestions. I prefer to share warm "feel good" messages with you, what I think of as the "heart stuff." Communication is more about head. It calls for logic and skill. Consistent daily and weekly communication empowers a team to be connected.

Everyone communicates. Few connect.

- J O H N   M A X W E L L

I encourage you to connect in meaningful ways that make others want to be around you. When we think about bringing people together, isn't it really about the heart?

In this chapter we will explore the many ways we communicate today and how to make the most of each of them. We'll look at everyday practices that lead to **good** communication. Because very few of us are satisfied with **good**, we'll look at how to take good communication and make it **better**. Ultimately, we'll discover the secrets to making your communication the **best** it can possibly be.

A good first step is to assess your current communication style and practices. How frequently do misunderstandings get in the way of relationships? To what extent do you feel connected to the people most important to you? How comfortable are you with your current approach to communication? I encourage you to be open and to look for areas that aren't working for you. I encourage you to *flip the switch*.

Verbal and nonverbal communication.

We communicate both verbally and nonverbally.

- **Verbal communication** is using language and words to convey a message. Sometimes we communicate in writing, and other times we communicate using our voice. They're both considered verbal communication. No matter your line of work, it likely involves a significant amount of verbal communication. Verbal communication can happen in one-on-one conversations, group interactions, and when one person speaks to a group.

- **Nonverbal communication** is what people see and feel when communicating in the presence of others. There have been several studies about nonverbal communication, and most experts agree that over half of all communication is nonverbal. To be fully understood, nonverbal communication calls for careful attention. Information can be conveyed through eye contact, facial expression, gestures, and tone. Carefully tuning in to what a person says and how they say it can give you clues about what a person is telling you.

Ms. Rapoza, my eighth grade Language Arts teacher, was a master communicator. Her distinctive style of verbal and nonverbal communication created a vibrant classroom atmosphere. She smiled constantly, and radiated sun-shining energy. She had an expressive face, and as she spoke, she punctuated each message with hand gestures. She masterfully chose the right words to inspire excellence in her students. When the class was working on a writing project, Ms. Rapoza would wander around the room. I remember her saying enthusiastically, "Joan, this is looking good! I can't wait to see your finished project!" She assumed I would do an excellent job, which inspired me to step up the quality of my work. Her combination of verbal and nonverbal communication, full of encouragement and positivity, always inspired me.

Whether you're building a personal relationship or building a business, strong communication skills are essential. When you connect verbally and nonverbally at the same time, you increase the chance that you will fully understand someone and their message. You also increase the chance that your message will be fully understood. You increase the likelihood that someone will take action.

How does team communication fit in?

Whether you are part of a team, leading a team, or both, you know that communication plays a major role in the way your team functions. Good communication allows you to be in a relationship, to set expectations, exchange ideas, solve problems, and connect as a group. Athletic teams, sales teams, and business teams can all benefit from improving the way they communicate.

> *The most important thing in communication is hearing what isn't said.*
>
> - PETER DRUCKER

Effective communication is best modeled from the top down. I have found that when I pay attention to what is and isn't working I've been able to provide my team with many *flip the switch* moments to improve. I currently lead a large network marketing team made up of sales leaders, sales professionals, and individuals who are new to the business. Like many teams today who function without the benefit of regular, face-to-face communication, we rely heavily on a variety of virtual tools and systems to stay connected. I am constantly striving to improve communication in my team. Technology with a personal touch has supported consistent connection. I am confident that the tools and systems that have worked for me will make a difference for you, no matter what environment you work in.

How important is listening?

Listening is essential to effective communication. Good listening goes well beyond hearing sounds; it's paying attention to what someone is saying and how they are saying it.

Have you ever noticed that you prefer to talk to people who listen well? They give you their full attention. Their expressions and words show you that no matter what you're saying, they're taking in your messages. They may even acknowledge what you're saying with words like:

- I hear you.
- I see you.
- You matter.
- I get it.
- I understand.

When someone is speaking, pay attention to what they're saying instead of thinking about how you'll respond. Listen. Acknowledge them. The best communicators are great listeners.

How do I make the most of the many ways we communicate today?

It's easy to convince ourselves that we are active and effective communicators when we keep up on email and reply to voice mail. Consistent communication calls for more than **responding** passively to incoming requests for your attention. The strongest communicators **initiate** communication with team members, clients, and associates.

When attempting to get someone's attention, it is crucial that you intentionally and repeatedly communicate key messages. A good communication strategy utilizes virtual tools in tandem with frequent, person-to-person communication. With today's many communication channels, it's best to send messages in a variety of ways, keeping in mind that not everyone uses the same tools.

- **Email**

  Billions of people use email today! It's great for sending longer communications, especially when you have one message to send to a group of people. It's simple, free, and especially effective for people who don't utilize social media platforms.

  I often use email to send messages to customers about special invitations, offers, or deadlines, and always follow up by individual texts and phone calls. With my team, I send a regular "All Team Email" at the same time every week. Being consistent in time of day and day of the week increases the likelihood that my messages will be read. I utilize regular email to recognize team successes, remind team members of upcoming deadlines and events, and provide short, motivational messages.

  I urge you not to overuse email. We receive so many emails these days that important messages can easily be overlooked. Consider, too, that email is not everyone's preferred way of communicating.

- **Text Messaging**

  Most of us check our phones frequently. Text messaging is a reliable way to make a quick connection because it's likely your message will be seen. One way to take a text message to a step above is to utilize voice texting. Many of today's apps have the option of recording a quick message instead of typing a text. You can personalize your message by including your positive energy and unique tone of voice.

  Texting can clearly communicate your message, but it is not two-way communication and should not be considered effective conversation. Texting is far from a perfect way to handle all communication needs, even when we insert emojis to convey emotion. Having said that, these are the most common ways I use text messaging:

- *Reminders:* I text quick reminders the evenings before a live group event or Zoom meeting. I know this works! On the rare occasion where I forgot to send a reminder, my attendance fell by as much as 33%. Because we all get busy, I frequently send text messages to remind of important dates and deadlines.

- *Arranging appointments:* When I want to schedule a phone conversation or one-on-one Zoom meeting with someone, I send a quick text to set up a time that will work for both of us. It's quick, easy, and gets the person thinking about our conversation ahead of time.

- *Quick applause:* We all like to know that our efforts are noticed, right? When I see an achievement that is worthy of applause, I text a quick "Way to go!" message until I'm able to make a phone call.

- **Telephone**

What I like best about the phone is that it's a two-way communication tool. Phone calls allow me to convey both my words and tone of voice. I can ask questions to tune in to the person I'm talking with. While I might begin a phone conversation with an intentional message, I am able to adjust and adapt based on how the conversation goes.

I recommend scheduling phone conversations. When you schedule a call, you won't lose precious time trying to chase someone down. I've noticed that people treat a scheduled appointment differently than an impromptu call. The scheduled call becomes a priority. Having a designated time on the calendar increases the likelihood that both parties will be focused on the conversation instead of the multi-tasking that often happens when we catch someone unprepared to talk. I also like the way a scheduled time helps a person think about our conversation before we even get on the phone.

It's important to get in the right frame of mind before you start a phone conversation. Remember that your tone of voice conveys your energy as much as it conveys your words. Start each call with positive energy; stay upbeat and you'll increase the likelihood that people want to talk with you.

- **Social Media Posts**

  I make daily use of social media to communicate with team members and customers. Posts are a great way to get information about what customers or teams need.

  - *Customer posts:* Consistent social media posts show customers you're open for business. Sometimes my customer posts are very specific, such as providing a product idea or alerting customers to a fantastic special. More often, though, I stay in touch in a friendly way to keep relationships active. Selling is a relationship business, right? I often post about things going on in my life without referring to the products I'm selling. I might share a vacation photo, a picture from a family get-together, or an inspirational message to brighten someone's day. Regular posts work well for interacting with customers, and they'll make your team members or employees feel connected to you.

- *Team posts:* I connect with several team groups through social media. While I know that social media posts aren't the only ways to be in touch, I make frequent use of team posts to stay connected. For example, I write a weekly message on Sunday nights to kick off the week in a positive way. After a live event or Zoom meeting, I post the recording. Within the body of my message, I encourage attendees to post their insights, questions, and ideas. When I review the post-meeting conversations, I can quickly assess what people are thinking and feeling, and identify future learning needs. While I use texting to send reminders, I use multiple communication forms to convey important messages.

- **Virtual Meeting Platforms**

  There are a number of platforms that facilitate face-to-face communication online, whether for a one-on-one conversation or a group meeting. Zoom is a great way for geographically distant groups to be together and a time-saver for local meetings. Because team members can actually see each other, I've noticed that our communication helps develop our team culture.

  The greatest advantage to me is that virtual platforms such as Zoom make it possible to engage both verbal and nonverbal communication. Because all participants appear on the screen, I can observe and react to facial expressions, how people are sitting, and their level of engagement. When someone seems disengaged or confused, I can ask them a simple question to immediately awaken their attention.

I utilize virtual meeting tools most often in these ways:

- *Training.* I have several recurring training meetings to target specific learning needs in my team. I provide a focused training event for new representatives, a separate training event for key performers, and a weekly event to support leaders. I enter each training event ready to present training content, equipped with discussion questions to inspire group interaction.

- *One-on-one conversations.* Because so much of communication is nonverbal, I know the importance of seeing a person's face as we're talking. Whenever possible, I utilize virtual conferencing for coaching conversations.

- **Digital Surveys**

  Surveys work well to poll team members about the ways they prefer to receive communication. Using Google Surveys or Survey Monkey, I ask questions to find out what's working well and what could work better. Many virtual communication companies, such as Constant Contact and Mail Chimp, have their own survey options.

  I might ask:

  - "What are the top two ways you prefer to receive messages?"
  - "How do you prefer to send messages?"

  I've noticed that participation increases when my survey questions are simple, in a multiple-choice format, or on a scale system. For example, I might ask, "On a scale of one to ten, how user-friendly is the new website?"

- **Face-to-face meetings**

  We have numerous ways to communicate, yet the tried-and-true face-to-face meeting remains the most effective way. Face-to-face meetings, whether one-on-one or in groups, engage all the senses and activate both verbal and nonverbal communication. In a group setting, one plus one often equals three ... in other words, there's an energy that builds when people are in the presence of others.

  Before the pandemic limited our ability to connect face-to-face, I regularly met customers and team members for coffee. I gathered my sales team for meetings that involved recognition, training, and motivation. Covid forced me to temporarily replace most of those contacts with regular phone calls or Zoom meetings, but I look forward to bringing live events back into the mix.

What are the best virtual tools today?

Communication tools are changing quickly, and new platforms are being developed every day. By the time you read this, there will likely be many new apps and platforms available for your use. Most of us are familiar with Facebook. At the time of writing, these are the additional tools I use most frequently:

- **Zoom**. This video conferencing platform allows you to connect online and has the advantage of verbal and nonverbal communication. Zoom is easy to learn, easy to use, and easy to share. It's definitely the platform I use most frequently.

- **Google Suite**. This provides one-stop shopping from email, to calendar, and meeting functions.

- **Voxer**. I love this because it's as if it puts a Walkie-Talkie at my fingertips whenever I want it. Voxer is a great tool to improve communication via voice messaging in real time. Voxer allows you to record short voice messages and send them through text messaging. Your energy, care, and personal touch come through with each message you send. My best tip is to keep all voice recordings under one minute to increase the likelihood that the recipient takes the time to listen.

- **Dropbox**. This gives you a way to store team or project files in one place. Dropbox is designed to reduce busywork, helps people stay focused, and is in sync with your team.

- **Trello**. This project management system helps people keep track of individual and shared projects in a well-organized way.

- **OneStream**. This provides pre-recorded streaming for live stream. It saves time and effort because it allows you to be in two remote places at once.

- **Mail Chimp**. While there are many tools available for sending, receiving, and managing email, Mail Chimp is a favorite. It's simple to set up and use. It's loaded with features that set it apart from standard email systems, such as the ability to distribute digital surveys. Mail Chimp also provides analytics that allow me to understand the open rate of a particular message, encouraging me to learn about what's working and what's not.

- **Cinch Share**. This program was created for the network marketing industry and helps sellers schedule their social media marketing messages. You can write and store your content and strategically schedule when you'd like each message to be released. It's a hassle-free tool that helps you make the most of social media platforms.

When it comes to using today's virtual tools, I recommend you choose one that works for you and stay with it. This will keep you from spending too much time learning the ins and outs of the different programs, leaving you more time to actually communicate!

What makes us avoid person-to-person communication?

Many of us have times where instead of taking action, we say, "I'll get to it tomorrow." As much as we know that communication is essential to our success, we occasionally procrastinate. What keeps us from initiating person-to-person communication more often?

- *Lack of confidence in the message*

  Let's say you have the idea to make phone calls to promote a special offer or to alert customers to exciting new products. You will feel better about making a phone call when you are confident in what you have to offer and convinced it's in your client's best interest to hear about it. If you doubt the real value of your offer, you'll lose confidence in your message. You might find yourself doing *anything* to avoid picking up the phone. Strengthen your belief in your offer before you reach out. Make a list of the benefits you're going to share. And consider this: Any time you plan to ask for something, whether it's an order, an appointment, or a commitment, be prepared to give something. You'll increase your confidence when you start from a place of serving others.

- *Not knowing what to say*

  Good communication involves getting clear about your messages ahead of time. Each month, I encourage leaders to choose three messages that are most important to communicate throughout the month. I recommend they start each one-on-one conversation, Zoom training, or social media live event by reinforcing these messages.

Leaders are often eager and excited to share solutions but not as eager to ask questions to get to the root cause of a problem. With increasingly frequent texts and emails, we easily get into the habit of telling instead of asking. What if in addition to thinking about what to say you thought about what to ask? You'll become a stronger communicator when you work on your questioning skills.

- *Lack of a simple communication strategy*

  Like many aspects of business, planning reduces stress and helps you get more done. A strong communication strategy increases the likelihood that you'll make contacts at consistent touch points. You'll utilize a variety of mediums to connect with more people. Your communication strategy will outline how you will use one-on-one conversations, emails, group contacts, reminders, and more.

One of the leaders I work with recently shifted her mindset about team communication. In one of our conversations about communication, I noticed she lacked confidence. She didn't have a communication strategy, which kept her from reaching her goal of growing a successful team and caused her undue stress. Prior to becoming a sales leader, her job was in a corporate environment where she managed a large number of people. The more we chatted, the more we realized that her past managerial role had caused her to form the habit of *telling* these people what to do. She had to learn that managing isn't the same as leading. She wasn't familiar with making phone calls to team members that were not just about what to do, but also about what was important to them.

When she stopped thinking about phone calls as a way to tell people what to do, she had a *flip the switch* moment. She learned to see phone calls as a way to be of service. I could hear her confidence getting stronger when she practiced saying, "What can I do for you today?" There was excitement in her voice when she talked about building and fine-tuning her communication strategy. Today her team is stronger. She's more confident and more satisfied with her business results. She has a plan to get in touch and stay in touch with her team. It's making a difference.

What could a simple communication strategy look like?

When I created a plan outlining ideal touch points, times, and spacing, it was easier to stay consistent in all of my communication efforts. I thought through my communication needs, my target audiences, and the ideal timing for making connections and then put it in writing. Communication is no longer something I simply aim to do each month. My communication strategy is a commitment to stay in touch because I know how much of a difference good communication makes to my relationships, my business, and to living a life I love.

> *The single biggest problem*
> *in communication*
> *is the illusion that it has taken place.*
>
> - GEORGE BERNARD SHAW

Joan's Network Marketing Communication Strategy
Good, Better, and Best

GOOD

- All-team email.
- All-team newsletter.
- Communicating company messages to the entire team.
- Email reminders for important dates, times, locations, and deadlines.

BETTER

- Small focus groups of like-minded individuals with common needs.
- Text reminders for important events and specials.
- Monthly calendars in a visible location. Tools such as LinkTree are a great way to store multiple links in one location.

BEST

- Be seen all over. When team members think of you, they'll think about their businesses.
- Be relatable.
- Schedule weekly time blocks to get to know employees or team members on a personal level.
- Make personal phone calls to recognize achievements. Each month, call your Top Ten achievers in defined performance categories.
- In-person meetings to evaluate goals and practices.
- Share communication strategy to inform and duplicate. Take a cascading approach, where you connect with top level first.
- Go live on social media team pages.

The BEST communication strategy is scheduled in advance. Use your calendar to stay consistent. I think of this as my "system," and it allows me to lay my head down at night feeling like I have supported the people who want and deserve the training I offer.

Is communicating the same as coaching?

Communicating is about consistently getting in touch and staying in touch with the people who are important to you. It's about sending and receiving messages as clearly as you can, remembering that we communicate both verbally and nonverbally. Good communication involves asking questions so you can fully understand another person's point of view, ideas, and challenges. Quality questions will generate quality answers. And good communication involves listening to what others **are** saying and noticing what they **aren't** saying.

As a sales leader, I am in conversations with team members every single day. Some conversations simply scratch the surface or convey an idea, a reminder, or encouragement to take action. In other conversations, my team members' needs might extend beyond what we are able to accomplish in a simple phone call. Through asking questions, I often uncover unmet needs, challenges, or goals that warrant a deeper discussion. When I notice that someone is looking for more, and willing to do more to get more, I know that they probably need coaching. I recommend a few scheduled coaching calls to take a deeper dive into what is most important to them.

It's important to make the distinction that while your *communication* efforts serve everyone on your team, *coaching* is for those people who have demonstrated they want more, and who have made a commitment to act to achieve personal and professional growth. When I was a new leader, one of the best tips I ever received to avoid beating my head against the wall was to match my time with a person's effort. Part of the art of being a leader is to identify the people who really want to build a business and deserve your investment of time. In Chapter Seven, we will explore how to identify those people, what coaching is, and how you can take steps to strengthen your coaching skills.

My experience has taught me to rise above what society is accepting and reach for more quality relationships in my life. Make the decision to communicate consistently—you'll feel more connected to the people who are important to you. You'll strengthen personal and business relationships and, if you are a leader, your team will grow stronger.

Life moves quickly these days. Without a strategy, you might unintentionally go days, weeks, and even months without contacting someone who is important to you. Make decisions about who you will connect with, how you'll connect, and when you'll connect. Pay attention to what a difference it makes to be a consistent communicator. Go from someone who reaches out only when it's easy. ***Flip the switch.*** Become a master communicator. Be in touch consistently with a clear message that informs, ignites, and inspires people to be more of who they are created to be.

SELF-COACHING QUESTIONS

Take time to assess the effectiveness of your communication. Be honest with yourself.

- What is my most commonly used method of communication? What draws me to this method? How confident am I that this method is effective?

- How would my team members and I benefit from using more communication channels?

- How often do I procrastinate when it comes to communication? What keeps me from communicating more consistently?

- Is my communication strategy good, better, or best? What will I do to improve? How will I use **Good**, **Better**, and **Best** to level up my communication strategy?

- Am I stronger at speaking or listening? What will I do to bring these into balance?

TAKE ACTION NOW!

It's time to elevate my communication skills!

- Take time to build a communication strategy and be mindful of the different target audiences you serve.

- Convert your communication strategy to a calendar so you maintain your commitment to consistent communication.

- Start a list of good questions you will ask when you're communicating with others. Keep building that list as you strengthen your communication skills.

- Share your communication strategy on your next leader call. Model it, teach it, and empower others to follow you.

MY THOUGHTS
AND REFLECTIONS

COMMUNICATE CONSISTENTLY

MY THOUGHTS
AND REFLECTIONS

COMMUNICATE CONSISTENTLY

CHAPTER SEVEN

PARTNER WITH A COACH SO YOU CAN COACH OTHERS

Coaching is unlocking a person's potential to maximize their own performance. It's helping them learn rather than teaching them.

- SIR JOHN WHITMORE

PARTNER WITH A COACH SO YOU CAN COACH OTHERS

oaching has played a major role in my life, on both a personal and professional level. I have increased my awareness, built my strengths, and navigated through many changes as the result of effective coaching. In this chapter, we will explore how coaching can help you create significant change in your life and in the lives of others.

In *Chapter Two, Manage Your Mindset,* we explored the concept of how self-coaching can increase our awareness and cause us to explore new ways of thinking. You may have noticed the "Self-Coaching Questions" that appear throughout this book. These are provided to equip you as you reflect upon what you are reading and to ignite your thought process. When you ask yourself good questions, you become more aware of what you are thinking and feeling. Self-coaching questions challenge you to become aware of your current reality.

When you know what you want, you can make the necessary changes that are important to you. Self-coaching helps you develop a deeper relationship with yourself, to begin the journey of accomplishing your dreams and goals. In my life, I have gained more clarity and focus by asking myself good questions.

As powerful as the practice of effective self-coaching can be, it has limitations. All of us are limited in our capacity to see ourselves. Further, it is not possible to be exceptional in all areas of life and business on our own. The best entrepreneurs, top performing athletes, and high-level executives have coaches. Seeking a coach is asking for help, which I see as a sign of strength. As an entrepreneur, the coaches I have worked with have helped me identify opportunities to improve, grow as a leader, and build confidence in my strengths.

If you want to take your life and business to the next level, hire a coach.

I have hired many coaches for different reasons over the past two decades. I can't think of a time when I didn't invest in coaching. Coaches have a way of guiding average performers to become great and top performers to reach their peak. Great coaches can connect and draw the most out of those they coach. Many of us don't see ourselves as truly capable of achieving greatness. By expanding personal and business skills, a coach can light our inner fires and help us become more of who we are created to be.

I prefer coaches who have mastered their skills or have been at the top of their profession, because they bring the insight gained by having achieved results. I especially appreciate when they are willing to hold me accountable. A good coach can see my blind spots, make me more aware, and guide me to move forward. A good coach inspires me to dig deeper and do a little more than I am comfortable doing.

The best coach I ever worked with was someone I heard speak at one of my company's sales conferences. She was poised and well prepared, and her training was impactful. She had built her own multimillion dollar sales organization, and explained success in a series of actionable steps. In a business where duplication is key, overcomplicating the basics is death to a team and company. Her training made it possible for others to go where she had gone.

She connected with her audience immediately by sharing a story about her early challenges. Everyone could identify with her story and could feel her beginning struggles, too. She had a kindness about her that radiated through the audience. She embodied confidence and wisdom that couldn't be missed. As I listened to her speak, I thought about what my dad had said: "Follow the best if you want to be the best." I knew right away that I wanted to learn from her, even though she didn't mention anything about being a coach. Websites didn't exist in those days. I recall running out the back door of the auditorium to grab a signed copy of her book and, hopefully, her phone number.

I was hungry to learn and grow. She had experience and strengths that I didn't—ones that I wanted to develop. That was twenty years ago, and I have coached with her over the years in multiple ways. She is now retired, yet I am frequently reminded of what I learned through coaching with her.

Experience great coaching to develop your own coaching skills.

When you are on the receiving end of a coaching relationship, you know how it feels to be coached. When you experience coaching, you become more able to strengthen your own coaching skills. Developing coaching skills will improve every area of your life. I am passionate about the skills used in coaching. They are simple skills. Yet, when practiced consistently, they will elevate people, teams, and companies to heights they never could have achieved. Like many skills, coaching skills develop through practice.

Looking back, the better my coaching skills became, the more people I could help in every way. My teams became healthier, team members were inspired to reach higher, and they stayed longer. By bringing coaching into my business approach, I was able to develop more six-figure earners on my team. I am frequently asked what I do to help so many develop multimillion dollar sales teams. One of my key strategies is to impact people by partnering one-on-one or in group coaching relationships.

The people who invest in coaching and coaching programs are more focused, more aware of blind spots, and are typically accountable to their coach. In my experience, the accountability alone has made coaching a worthwhile experience. Being accountable to a coach has kept me on track and moving toward my goals on days when I didn't feel like taking action. I would not be where I am today without a coach or by learning and practicing the skills of coaching.

Partner with people who have a true desire to learn and grow.

I have learned to identify people who demonstrate a strong desire for personal and professional growth. At first I thought that the most motivated people on my team were the ones who talked the most about moving forward. Instead, I discovered that I needed to pay attention to more than words. Without the right actions behind them, words are just ideas. I study and evaluate business results and notice the extent to which someone takes action on the things they talk about. Execution is key to accomplishing any goal.

> *The biggest difference between successful people and unsuccessful people is that successful people are willing to do what unsuccessful people are not.*

- DARREN HARDY

When I coach people, I help them think about what they want. I work with them on business-building principles, mindset, and strategy. I bring them to the edge of discomfort. And then I lean in a little more. This is done effectively by getting to know them (heart) and recognizing their skill level (head). This is why one-stop coaching rarely produces long-term results. One session might help someone become aware or even overcome a specific challenge, but I find that it takes multiple sessions and commitment by the one being coached to work on herself and create lasting change.

Trust your intuition. You are usually right.

A team member I didn't know very well told me she wanted to take her business to the next level. I saw a spark in her eye. My intuition told me she had a strong desire to learn and grow, but I needed to look more deeply to determine the extent to which I wanted to invest my time in working closely with her.

Her sales numbers showed me she had strong sales skills, but I saw she did not fully understand strategy. That wasn't uncommon. I noticed she was *leaving money on the table*. I knew she didn't realize how much more money she could be making and that I could help her get focused and working in the right areas with her team. I needed to know her better before I could begin to coach her. I complimented what I saw in her and asked a lot of questions. People need to feel your interest in them. My sincere interest in her showed her I cared. Kindness will make more of a difference than any skill I have learned.

Relationships start by being interested in people.

She allowed me to dig more deeply to get to the root of some of her tender feelings. I have heard it said that you have to *offer a hand to touch a heart*, and I find this to be true. Relationships take time. Developing people takes time. I invited her to my hometown to help her accelerate the process. We got to know each other, and before long, I was coaching with her. She had the willingness and desire to grow. The right people are easy to work with. Our relationship got stronger with each interaction. By discovering her personality, uncovering her "why," and learning what was important to her, I was able to quickly guide her to navigate her challenges. Over time, she developed the skills and confidence that equipped her to realize many of her goals.

When you don't know someone within your team or you are not familiar with their business trends, study their numbers and ask questions. I try to become familiar with their results over the previous 90 days and look for the trends. Without meeting them, I can usually determine whether they are go-getters and identify opportunities to help them.

- Identify who is **hungry**, who is **willing**, and who has **desire**.
- Study trends: numbers, habits, and results.
- Look for a pattern of consistency.
- Do they attend trainings and meetings?
- Are they kind?

- Do they have a great attitude?
- New team members and emerging leaders are priorities, and require conversations.

Invite people to coach with you based on what you see and what they do. You will quickly learn whether they're ready for coaching.

Know when it's time to let go of a coaching relationship.

I remember a time when my coach asked me, "Joan, why do you think you are successful?" I thought about her question, and quickly rattled off a myriad of answers. We talked about each of them, and she asked whether I wanted her feedback. Of course, I said, "Yes!" She went on to say, "You are successful, in part, because you know how to gracefully cut the cord." She noticed that I knew who to coach, who not to coach, and when it was time to let go of a coaching relationship. I posted her words on my desk for years as a reminder of who to coach and how long to coach. We can love everyone, but that doesn't mean everyone needs the same level of attention and training.

In those days I didn't even think about the fact that one of the biggest roadblocks to a successful business is working with the wrong people for too long and expecting different results. Sometimes people aren't coachable; sometimes they just don't want it. By asking quality, open-ended questions, you can determine who the right people are.

You are likely acquainted with the Pareto Principle, commonly referred to as the 80/20 rule. Summarized, this principle says that 80% of effects (output) come from 20% of causes (inputs). I remind my leaders of the 80/20 rule: 80% of the people are doing a little business here and there, and these team members ***do not*** benefit from coaching. The remaining 20% are active business-builders and leaders, and these are the people you ***do*** want to invite to coach with you. When you understand this rule at play in your business, you understand that you don't have to coach everyone.

When a coaching relationship isn't working for you, it probably isn't working for the person you're coaching, either. It doesn't have to feel confrontational if you set expectations at the beginning of the coaching relationship. If you are in a coaching relationship where the one you're coaching isn't growing and you feel like you are pulling them along, or it feels more important to you than to them, it could be time to gracefully cut the cord. I have learned that you can dissolve a coaching relationship kindly and honestly with clear communication.

I believe I am always working with the right people at the right time. This is part of what makes me love what I do. I can coach someone whether I'm in my home office or on a beach in Maui. As I coach others to live a life they love, I fully enjoy the life I have created.

Learning and growing as a coach

After years of coaching my team members, I realized that I truly enjoy helping others make life-changing discoveries about themselves. I find great joy in guiding someone to overcome challenges and become more. I decided to invest in a formal coach training program to become a Professional Certified Coach. I was determined to learn and refine this skill.

Coaching Training Programs develop core competencies and provide structured practice, observation, and comprehensive review before awarding the designation of "Certified Coach." My training program was challenging, and the skills I learned did not come naturally. It took practice (*lots* of practice!) before I felt comfortable. I recall a facilitator who effortlessly helped people out of their limiting beliefs. I wanted to have those skills. I practiced relentlessly every chance I had. Over time and with focused practice on my skills, it has become second nature to help someone let go of a limiting belief.

I learned about coaching by being coached, by making coaching conversations a major part of my approach to leading a sales team, and through a professional training program. I continue to learn about coaching through practice.

How to conduct a coaching call

Time is your most limited resource. I can usually conduct an effective coaching call in 30-45 minutes. Practice has taught me to make the most of every precious minute I spend on a coaching call.

The ***30-Minute Coaching Call Outline*** on page 166 shows you what a call might look like. Use this as a starting point to guide the flow of your coaching conversations. You may need to adjust time based on the needs and time constraints of the person you're coaching.

30-Minute Coaching Call

TIME	OBJECTIVE	INTRODUCTION	TACTIC
5 Minutes	**Connect**	*"What's going on today in your world?"*	• Light, non-business conversation • Small talk kicks off the call.
5 Minutes	**Celebrate**	*"Specifically, what's going well?"*	• Positive energy sets the tone. • Celebrate successes!
5-10 Minutes	**Objectives**	*"What three objectives would you like to accomplish?"*	• Ask for three. • Ask which is most important. • Start there.
5-10 Minutes	**Challenges**	*"Which challenges/ road blocks are you facing?"*	• Validate. • Ask clarifying questions. • Move forward to solution.
5 Minutes	**Take Action Now**	*"What are your next steps?"*	• End with three action steps. • Give a due date for them to get back to you with progress.

> *Each person holds so much power*
> *within themselves*
> *that needs to be let out.*
> *Sometimes they just need*
> *a little nudge,*
> *a little direction,*
> *a little support,*
> *a little coaching,*
> *and the greatest things can happen.*

- PETE CARROLL

Joan's Top "8" Coaching Tips

1) **Invite a qualified participant to partner with you.**

   Often your best coaching candidates don't know that you see so much in them and want to work closely with them.

2) **Set expectations for a coaching relationship.**

   We all feel better when we know what is expected.

3) **Request a coach preparation worksheet.**

   Ask that it is returned at least 24 hours prior to your first coaching conversation. This helps both parties to be prepared.

4) **Ask open-ended questions: Who, what, where, when and how.**

   Watch out for dead-end, or yes/no, questions. They keep your conversation from moving forward. See Page 10 for my favorite coaching questions.

5) **Listen.**

   Jot down what the person you're coaching says, so you pay more attention to what they're saying than to what you're going to say next.

6) Compliment what you see in them.

What did you notice when you reviewed their results? What characteristics have you noticed that suggest success? Let those you're coaching know that you're paying attention.

7) Ask permission to hold someone accountable to their dreams and goals.

By asking permission, you open the door to follow up conversations about what they say they want to accomplish.

8) End with a focus on action steps.

Those you're coaching may naturally share the action steps they plan to take. You might choose to add a few suggestions that will move them closer to their goals. The key is to end all coaching calls with a call to action!

How is coaching different from training?

Coaching and training are often misunderstood. People tend to think they are coaching when they are training, and vice versa. While there is some overlap in skills, let's look at some of the differences.

Coaching is about the game plan of the person you are coaching. Coaching conversations revolve around what they want to accomplish.

- Coaching is an agreed-upon partnership between two people.
- Coaching is a conversation intended to take a person where she can't take herself.
- Coaching is pulling things out of a person, rather than filling up a person.
- Coaching is listening and responding, not telling and reacting.
- Coaching is a relationship built on principles of caring, safety, and trust.

Training is about the trainer's game plan. You train to build a skill or transfer your knowledge.

- Training is the transfer of knowledge from one to another, or one to many.
- Training informs, delivers knowledge, and teaches skills.
- Training is logical. Great training is easy to follow using principles, methodology, steps, and strategy.
- Training is a prepared subject on a skill or strategy to elevate a result.
- Training is filling someone up, rather than drawing out of a person.

There is no doubt that coaching has made a major difference in my life and in my success. *Self-coaching* has taught me to think constructively. *Being coached* has inspired me to think differently about myself and my actions. *Coaching others* has become an essential part of my leadership strategy and provided tremendous personal gratification. It is very satisfying to help others experience the breakthroughs that inspire and equip them to achieve their goals. I delight each day in seeing people *Flip the switch* and experience the life they love.

When you build your coaching skills, you will see an impact in every area of your life and business. Whether you are an experienced leader or just starting out, getting better at coaching takes time. With time, coaching will become a natural part of what you do. Be patient. Be gentle with yourself, and keep practicing.

Learn the art of asking good questions.
Download this today to immediately improve
your coaching skills:

Quality Questions for Better Coaching Conversations

www.joanrobison.com/QualityQuestionsforBetter
CoachingConversations

MY THOUGHTS
AND REFLECTIONS

‿♡‿

....

....

....

....

....

....

....

....

....

....

....

....

....

....

....

....

....

....

....

....

....

....

PARTNER WITH A COACH SO YOU CAN COACH OTHERS

MY THOUGHTS
AND REFLECTIONS

PARTNER WITH A COACH SO YOU CAN COACH OTHERS

CHAPTER EIGHT

LEADERSHIP AND EMPOWERMENT

If your actions inspire others to dream more, learn more, do more, and become more, you are a leader.

- JOHN QUINCY ADAMS

LEADERSHIP AND EMPOWERMENT

Leadership is the process of impacting and influencing others in significant ways. Managing is about accomplishing **tasks**. Leading, on the other hand, is about building **people**. The best leaders create a vision and help others see possibilities they may have never considered.

In this chapter, we will focus on how to lead through empowering and developing others. We will call back ideas from past chapters. Much like other skills, your leadership skills will develop over time and with practice. Know that helping a person grow and develop skills is one of the best gifts you can give them. Meanwhile, leading is tremendously gratifying to you, too. The joy I feel when I see someone break through is one of the best feelings in the world.

I encourage you to be open to evaluating where you are in your leadership growth. The best leaders are never done growing. Have the courage to ask yourself questions about how well you lead others. Be open to building strength as a leader.

Show people you care before trying to lead them.

If you've ever heard the term "servant leader," it refers to a leader who embodies the principle of serving others through leading them.

Servant leaders care for the people they lead. What do you think inspires people to work with you? Is it position or title? Is it policies and procedures? Or is it knowing that you, their leader, truly care for them?

People don't care how much you know until they know how much you care.

- THEODORE ROOSEVELT

Nordstrom was founded in 1901 by John Nordstrom and Carl Wallin, and their commitment to customer service has never wavered. If you were to ask most anyone what Nordstrom is known for, they would say, "customer service." Nordstrom cares about the people they serve.

The foundation on which Nordstrom was built was to hire people who would best serve their customers. Nordstrom took a "test drive" approach to hiring new associates. Most team members would be hired during a sale, on a part time basis, starting at entry level positions such as a stock person or cashier. Based on several performance factors, employees would be called back to work another sale, permanently hired, or thanked for their time.

The way Nordstrom treated its customers was the same way they treated their employees. Pete Nordstrom was the store manager of one of the Nordstrom stores where I worked for several years. After morning announcements, Pete would make his rounds and walk around the store to connect with employees in each department and greet them with a smile. He knew the names of the employees and made it a point to make each of them feel special.

I believe a big part of the employee longevity was that people felt they were part of the Nordstrom family. Nordstrom's approach to leadership was to care for the people who made them a company:

their customers and the associates who served them. Pete Nordstrom made a difference. He continues to show strength in leadership. Today Pete serves as Nordstrom's Co-President.

To connect with people and show them you care:

- Take a few minutes and get to know the people you lead. Ask questions about their day, their family, or weekend. Be sincerely interested.

- Make them feel good about what they are doing. Remind them frequently of the importance of their work.

- Make personal phone calls. Make recognition calls to top performers.

- Recognize people as often as you can. Make frequent use of one-on-one meetings and Zooms. Highlight people by name in blogs or newsletters.

- Give team members a feeling of ownership by having them collaborate on committees and in small groups. Companies don't succeed unless the employees buy into the company's principles and practices.

- Include team members as you plan initiatives and new rollouts. Including others will make them feel appreciated and valued.

Believe in people before they believe in themselves.

I have observed that it is during challenging times most growth is experienced. Difficulties often cause people to ask for help. People are often more coachable and open to suggestions during challenges. Many of the people I have coached appreciate hearing what I see in them, because often it is what they do not yet see in themselves. Consider these ways to show your people you believe in them:

- Listen.
- Encourage.
- Speak truth.
- Challenge.
- Walk with your people.

Your words of encouragement will often make an imprint on another person's heart and change the direction of their life in a positive way.

Effective Leadership begins with "E."

It is important that leaders don't become comfortable and complacent but that they remain engaged in the journey of growing as leaders. It helps to find different ways to measure the effectiveness of your leadership. Below you will see five words that describe leaders I admire. One way I measure leadership effectiveness is to keep these words on an index card and periodically evaluate where I am and how I can improve. This keeps me on my toes!

1. **Empathy** is essential to insight and understanding. Empathy doesn't mean you agree with a person's point of view; it means you understand it. It is the ability to rise above your own thoughts in each situation. By focusing on caring for someone's needs, you have greater impact. Leaders who develop the skill of being empathetic create more loyal followers and build stronger relationships.

2. **Encouraging.** An encouraging word gives a person the emotional fuel to take the next step. It's amazing how little time it takes to encourage someone. Focusing on peoples' strengths results in greater self-confidence and higher performance levels. Your encouragement can make people feel noticed, cared for, and valued.

3. **Equipping** is preparing people by teaching them the skills they need to succeed. Equipping others is a vital component of developing leaders. We can't equip our people with what we don't have. Training others reinforces our own skills and keeps us growing.

4. **Endurance** builds character and strengthens the leader. Endurance is needed when the road gets long as challenges occur. A great leader shows how to take a pause, or even a fall, and get back up again. A great leader shows how to keep momentum going, regardless of detours. Often the greatest challenges build the most endurance and strength in a leader. Smart leaders use challenges as tools to equip their people.

5. **Empowering** others is giving them the reins to take on projects and make decisions. Empowering leaders doesn't mean you turn everything over without a thought or plan. Checking in to measure progress is important for learning. A great leader knows that if she has equipped her people for the journey, she can trust and let go. By empowering others, you produce strong leaders and a well-rounded team culture of multiplying leaders.

Let go so others can grow.

When it comes to overseeing a task or project, it can be challenging for some leaders to relinquish control. Letting go is a growth opportunity for the leader. As a business or team grows, we often aren't developing leadership in others at the rate of the business' growth. Some leaders are accustomed to doing everything themselves and can easily fall into the trap of thinking that only they can do the work. This mentality is detrimental to scaling even a small business.

There are times when you think you've empowered others when, in fact, they may not be fully equipped. In the fullness of a week, training someone to do the entire job or project can take more time than a leader allocates. I find walking them through the process has proven to be most effective. As a leader, this becomes essential when my primary work involves building other leaders. The quality of developing a leader step-by-step is important to learning and applying what they know. At times, giving too much too soon with a sink or swim mentality doesn't set up the emerging leader to win. The result will fall short of the leader's expectation. This makes perfect sense as to why a leader may not want to let go. An effective empowerment approach is to intentionally train one skill at a time and measure results before introducing another skill. Consider *flipping the switch* slowly; often, new leaders will have fresh ideas and insight.

I was working closely with a hard-working leader on my team, and recognized that she was burning the candle at both ends. She continually commented that she wished for more hours in the day. I could relate because I, too, have been prone to fall into this trap. Adding more to your plate increases priorities. With more priorities, quality of production usually suffers.

One day after hitting a wall, she asked, "Why aren't some of the leaders on my team stepping up like I did?" She quickly realized that by doing for them, they didn't have a reason to step up. In a few coaching sessions we were able to identify areas where she could empower emerging leaders and let go of some responsibilities. She later learned that a few of the leaders had experience in ways that she didn't. By empowering others, she was clearly seeing multiple benefits. What started as fear turned out to be a great lesson in *flipping the switch*.

Empowerment calls for honest feedback.

Leaders are often placed in the position of evaluating someone's effort. Whether you are in a debriefing session, evaluating someone's performance, or taking stock of the work product produced by a team member, be courageous and take the high road. Provide concrete, honest feedback. If the work you are evaluating is not ideal, have a caring, yet frank, conversation. If you worry too much about whether your honest feedback will cause hurt feelings, you will keep others from growing. Deliver truth respectfully and with grace. Kindness matters. You are a leader, and leaders build people.

People want the truth. They don't want to be left in the *dark*. They may not always like the truth, but speaking the truth is the right thing to do for others. The truth is the *light*. Great leaders shine the light among their people.

Leading starts with authentic modeling.

Leading is a way of being. I am still learning how to be a better leader. I have had my share of challenging times when I felt defeated, but not for long. Leaders dust themselves off and get back up. I won't give up working on myself or developing leaders.

Early in my career I realized that I needed to be the kind of leader I wanted to attract to my team. Thinking back to Chapter One, where my dad told me to follow the best to be the best, I have taken advantage of every leadership training opportunity that has been made available to me. I'm always learning by observing the practices of successful leaders and simply doing what they do. One thing that the leaders I admire have in common is they keep working on themselves. They continue to attend training on topics that they already know with a fresh set of eyes, often finding nuggets they did not hear before. They participate in company-hosted events and seek out opportunities to keep developing personally.

How do you follow the best to be the best? Do you take advantage of every learning opportunity that is made available to you? Sometimes you need a meeting. Sometimes a meeting needs you. Often, both are true.

A leader will attract more people and establish a healthy team culture when the leader models real life authenticity. The leader becomes more likable and approachable. This requires the leader to let her guard down and leave "picture perfect" at the door. When you are an authentic leader, you are relatable. You show you're human. Model authenticity in your team by sharing common challenges through stories and inspiration.

> *Alone, we can do so little ...*
> *... together,*
> *we can do so much.*
>
> - HELEN KELLER

When a team member thinks about a story you shared, she may be inspired to dig a little deeper. I continue sharing many of my greatest challenges of being in the dark with the hope of helping others act in the face of fear. My reach has expanded because I am not afraid to be vulnerable. I believe one of the greatest gifts of leadership is giving others the benefit of the person you have become.

Get people into motion with accountability.

Most people who aren't moving forward are experiencing a level of fear. As we learned in Chapter Three, the quickest way out of fear is to get out of self and get in motion. As the leader, it's up to you to ignite action in others. It's not empowering to fix problems for people. How would that support the person's growth? Instead of being the one to get in motion, inspire the motion within your team members. I learned the hard way that when I was the one in motion, I was taking a growth opportunity away from someone else. I learned to *flip the switch* from enabling to empowering.

Getting people in motion calls for more than telling them what to do. It works well to involve people in their solutions. People rarely argue with their own ideas. It is easier to get someone in motion when they are open and coachable. Blend your coaching and training skills to empower others. Get your people into forward motion by:

- **Connecting** and showing you care.
- **Asking and listening** to give you insight and allow them to think.
- **Leading them** by showing what is possible with forward motion and what can happen without forward motion.
- **Offering** suggestions to get into motion.
- **Asking** them what they will do. When will they have this done? What part can they do now or today?

To inspire a person into forward motion, inspire a feeling of urgency. Urgent action keeps fear from taking root. Ask someone to commit to a deadline and you will move people into action urgently. As we learned in Chapter Three, Overcome Your Fears, the mind chooses to sit with fear over experiencing it. It's more comfortable. Getting people into forward motion elevates confidence, creates space for wins, and builds winning teams.

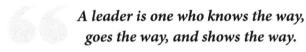

A leader is one who knows the way, goes the way, and shows the way.

- JOHN MAXWELL

Shine a light on the big picture.

Think about climbing a mountain. The ultimate goal is to climb to the top of the mountain, learn from the experience, and enjoy the journey. The journey is not one that we arrive at but an ongoing path of growth. The person we become along the way is the most important part of the journey. Being in the moment while enjoying the journey didn't come easily to me. For me, a key to living in the "now" has been practicing looking for the good and just "being."

There will be setbacks, pauses, and areas to take in the majestic views. Big-picture thinking is important in choosing a path of possibility. It also serves as inspiration when we get stuck on the mountain. I've not met a person who, at times, was free from the emotional detours that distracted her from the big picture. Things out of our control can't be avoided. Ideally, we learn along the journey that detours don't have to derail us. They are meant to teach us.

As we increase our awareness of the ways we work with our people, we notice that people develop at different paces. There are times when we need to shine the light on what is possible to inspire them to take the next step. Other times, it is necessary to remind them of the real reason they are doing the daily and weekly tasks. For others, letting them find their way is necessary. Space is needed before they begin to climb again.

Pause and think about the big picture. Do you know where you are going? How are you shining the light on the path for others?

A friend once asked me a profound question. He asked, "Joan, what is the meaning of your life?" I had dreams and goals and was not a stranger to mapping out my plans to achieve them. And yet the word "meaning," as it related to the substance of my life, was something I had not yet given much thought to. The question nearly took my breath away.

I answered, "The meaning of my life is to help people." I didn't forget the question. My answer seemed broad, and the question continued to nag me. Our conversation caused me to dig deeper and search my heart. I wasn't sure I really knew the meaning of my life. In prayer, I asked God to shine the light on more of what the *meaning of my life* looked like from His vantage point. I wanted the bird's-eye view. Knowing where you are going is important, especially as we lead people. Shining a light on the big picture and the meaning behind it has brought more clarity to the choices I make in my daily habits.

Big-picture thinking can shine a light on a goal and illuminate its importance. It can be reminding someone of the meaning behind a campaign to raise money for a particular cause. Showing the big picture can be shining a light on what you see in a person and helping them see what is possible for them. Great leaders do this by seeing the big picture and creating a shared vision in their teams.

The book *Flip **The** Switch* started with a simple idea: how can I help more people out of fear? Many challenges that were met along the way were tackled by knowing the big picture. On days where I felt weary or like quitting, people appeared in unexpected ways to encouraged me. My friend, Tom, always tells me, "The big picture is always perfect."

Leadership matters today. We are adapting to changes everywhere, and we want leaders who have been where we want to go. We want leaders who care enough to help us become our best selves. Leaders show the way. You can be the leader someone needs to live a life they love.

It isn't easy to develop your strengths in leadership. It takes heart. It takes mind. It takes work. With time and practice you will see the rewards. Leadership starts with you. It returns to you. Empowering and developing others is one of the most challenging, yet rewarding, opportunities I've been given.

You are on a journey to building your leadership strength. Enjoy what you are learning. Enjoy the relationships you build with the people you are privileged to lead. Remind yourself that the work you do is significant. It matters. As a leader, you empower and develop people to transform their lives. To live a life they love. And that matters.

Would you like to increase your effectiveness in building leaders? Download this easy-to-follow printable tip sheet today:

Top 5 Tips to Develop Leaders

www.joanrobison.com/Top5TipstoDevelopLeaders

SELF-COACHING QUESTIONS

Be open to evaluating your current approach to leadership. Think about ways to grow stronger and become more effective every day.

- Which of the five "E" leadership qualities is my current strength? How will I continue to build on that strength?

- On which of the "E" leadership qualities will I focus my attention this week? What will I do to strengthen that quality in myself?

- As a leader, in which situations is it hard for me to let go of control? What will I do to focus my energies on empowering others?

- What can I do this week to shine a light on the big picture?

- What makes it difficult for me to be truthful when providing feedback? What will I do to remind myself that my role calls for respectful, graceful truth so I can help others grow?

TAKE ACTION NOW!

It's time to get moving and put to work what you have learned.

- Choose and connect with three people on your team. Be intentional about showing them you care.

- Who needs you to help them get in motion this week? When will you reach out and help them out of fear and into action?

- Practice an honest feedback session with a friend to increase your confidence the next time you step into an actual feedback session.

- Write in your journal. Reflect on what empowerment means to you. Write about the ways you want to build strength as a leader.

MY THOUGHTS
AND REFLECTIONS

LEADERSHIP AND EMPOWERMENT

MY THOUGHTS
AND REFLECTIONS

LEADERSHIP AND EMPOWERMENT

CONCLUSION

Change isn't easy. It takes work to improve your life. It is my hope that *Flip The Switch* has opened your eyes to new possibilities.

- If there are aspects of your life that need cleaning up, tap into your courage to clean them up one thing at a time. You'll be glad you did.

- Mind your mindset. Create new rituals that help you start each day with the fuel you need to take on any challenge.

- Overcome your fears. Instead of waiting for fear to go away, nudge yourself to take action, even in the presence of fear. You will learn and grow.

- Connect with your source of strength by praying. Meditate so you can listen. Love others because love is what life is all about.

- Have a heart for people. Show them you care.

- Communicate. When you stay in touch, you build relationships.

- Partner with a coach. Sometimes you need a little help and encouragement to become your best self.

- Lead the way and empower others. Experience joy as you make a difference in the lives of people you work with.

Is it time for you to *flip the switch* to ignite transformational change? It's up to you. Tap into your energy, your strength, and your desire to create a life you love.

ACKNOWLEDGEMENTS

This book would never have been possible without the love, support, expertise, and encouragement of many.

I am endlessly grateful to my parents, Wayne and Marcia Carslin. On the days where words didn't come, I felt you there. The days when words came, I felt you there. Our physical days may be of the past, but your presence is felt in every day. You are still my first "go-to." Thank you for never leaving. I love you.

Thank you, Dad, Roger Nilsen, for showing me every day how it looks to fight the good fight. I learned how to be a woman of character by following your example. Thank you to my other mom, Becky Nilsen, for all you do for our family and the love that you show me daily. Thank you. I love you both beyond what I can describe.

Thank you to my son, Miles Nilsen. You are my greatest teacher. Some of my toughest decisions in this life were made because of you. You are tender, strong, and wise beyond your years. You light the world on fire. Thank you for choosing me to be your mom. Thank you for your patience as I spent hours on the phone and working. I know that today you can see I chose this profession for YOU. Being there for you was one of the strongest desires of my heart. I think we did a damn good job! Teamwork!

Thank you to the Nilsen family of entrepreneurs. You were born to love and lead and born to serve. We are Nilsens.

Grandpa Carl and Grandma Irene Nilsen, you are missed every day. Your lessons, love, and stories are alive in your legacy!

Thank you, Ms. Randi Rapoza, for shining your light on your students and me. YOU were the first teacher that made me want to be better! I love you!

Thank you to my beautiful friends, Steve and Sally. The example you showed of loving each other taught me so much!

Thank you, Ms. Cynthia Eady. Your support then and now means so much to me. The first day of your class you shined the light of God's love for us all to see. I love you!

My Dearest Dee Little! What can I say … we were years apart, and yet our age never mattered a thing. God sure knew … I can't believe we both had such similar stories. From working at the cinemas to our love for the Lord! You touched my heart, Dee, in a way where I never felt judged and oh … what mess I was. I miss you so much, but know you are exactly where you always wanted to be … with your Father! Love never dies. Until I see you face to face … I will keep on keeping on! Fighting the good fight! I love you!

Thank you to Sue Rusch, my mentor, coach, and content editor. I thank you for giving your best to me so I can give my best to others. Thank you for shining your light on me then and now. I can't believe this is your LAST project … LUCKY me! Enjoy retirement! I love you lady!

Thank you, Jenn Fort, for being my right arm. I can't thank you enough. Thank you for the early mornings and late nights and all the FUN we have in-between! Thank you for continuing to smile as you heard the words, "Hi, Jenn, it's Joan." Thank you for your patience with my endless stream of rapid-fire conversations, whether they were the first or the fiftieth one in a day. Thank you, sweet one, for everything you do to make me look good. Everyone needs a Jenn in their life! I love you!

Thank you to Tony Ferraro. Coaching with you has kept me on my toes! Thank you for challenging me and believing in me.

Thank you, Rodrigo Rodriguez, for always being there for me. I am grateful for your commitment to the family! You are the BEST father ever, Miles is so blessed to have a dad like you! I couldn't ask for anything more. I love you always.

Thank you to my friend, Tom, for being a great example. The big picture is perfect.

Thank you to Connie and Dave for all of your support and care on this journey of life. You have never wavered. I love you!

My appreciation and adoration run deep for you, Bri! Thank you, Brian Nilsen, for always standing by me and believing in me. I am so proud of you and all you've accomplished! We have come a long way since the days of Surfrest Park. I love you, Sissy! P.S. Oh, and thank you for never pushing me in the water. (Ha ha!)

Sarah Nilsen, thank you for giving me the push when I need it and knowing when I need it. Thank you for being the funny one who keeps us rolling our eyes at ourselves! Thank you for the days where we got a hot idea and worked until we couldn't see. Thank you for the days where we crushed it. I will always remember the days where I made you walk into random establishments with our products. HA HA! Thank you for the vacations, the beaches, and all the family events. Life is better with YOU in it! I love you sissy!

Talia and Theodore Vandegrift, thank you for understanding Gigi was "writing" for months. Even though it seemed like years. LOL! Talia, I am so proud of the mother you are. Theodore is one lucky boy. Well done, TT. I love you so much.

Melissa, thank you for being my best friend since we were twelve years old. Always there. We have logged some hours, haven't we? From working together to doing life together, the stories, fun, and all the in between! WOW! How lucky am I?!? Many things will remain in the vault. HA! HA! Thank you for introducing me to the amazing network marketing industry. Your invitation changed the trajectory of my life. Forever, I love you.

Thank you, Deanna Bowman, you have been walking my journey with me since 2001. Two very different women collide, and viola, they were more the same than they thought! AMAZING how God works in our lives. I love reminiscing and seeing how God used both of us, for each other, in such different ways. You have been a friend, a mentor, and a partner. I can't thank you enough for always praying for me and being there! I love you!

Tracy Rodgers, the first Diamond National! Thank you for the invite! Who would've thought our paths would continue to cross? The support and love you give shines through. I get chills seeing God work the amazing in our lives. CAN'T make this stuff up! xo

Thank you, Rob Sperry, for writing me the beautiful foreword. Truly, you are the master networker and the master at loving people where they are. Thank you for all the coaching and answering ALL my questions! You have a calm patience blended with wisdom and knowledge that is so admirable! Your example in business and loving your family is such a gift to witness for people today. Keep shinning your light, Rob!

To my key leaders, Kristie DeMenna, Risa Garrett, and Megan Miles, I appreciate you all so very much! When a leader is away and their team runs beautifully without them, it is a sign of amazing leadership. YOU are the glue that makes us amazing! Thank you for being the amazing leaders you are. I am grateful for your partnership and trust in me over the last four years and staying the course. You have built amazing teams and developed into incredible leaders. Each of you brings a tear of joy to my eye. I am so proud of the culture we have created. I love doing life every day with you.

To Brandie & Ginna and the amazing social marketing team! Our reach is far and wide. Thank you for your fabulous, creative ideas and commitment to our team. All the Zooms, all the time spent… We are igniting more light every day.

I am beyond grateful to the mentors and coaches who have stuck by me and given me guidance and encouragement on my journey. Your commitment to me gave me courage every step of the way.

Thank you to the thousands of team members who partnered with me and allowed me to support you. It has been an honor to work with you and always my pleasure.

Thank you, Nicki Keohohou, the master of all masters of network marketing coaches! YOU taught me so much … the skills, coaching principles and all the words and questions in between. Being a certified coach and trainer has changed my life. I am so appreciative of you and your dream. Love you, Nicki!

Malvika, I am so grateful for ALL your time and commitment to me, to my journey through this life! Your guidance and partnership have meant so much to me. After all these years it's a beautiful thing when a mentor becomes a beautiful friend. I love ya, Mal!

To Mary, thank you for the hours of listening and mentoring me. You taught me the words, "What I love about me," and I am grateful. I feel your brilliance every time I am in a room with you! XO

To Tera, thank you for tuning me up and in. ALL your encouragement through the bumps … I can't thank you enough! Those times … well, good to know I am not crazy. A little bit… HA HA! Your constant light is a gift to the world and me.

Cynthia, thank you for your kindness, care, and guidance and all the adjustments. I have loved getting to know you over the past year. You have helped me more than you know!

Thank you for being my Voxer bestie, Dani Fryer, whoop whoop! When two people click together like you knew them forever! YOU are that person!

Thank you, Kim Fisher, for all the walks, the talks, and knowing just how to get me out of my house … LOL! I love our friendship and time we spend. YOU shine bright! I love you!

To Liliana Gonzalez Garcia, thank you! Where do I begin to express my appreciation for your patience, design expertise, and willingness to do whatever it takes? I'm grateful for YOU.

To my family at Nordstrom's, Sensaria, Votre Vu, and Color Street, thank you. My experience in being part of each family has given me the confidence to share what I have learned in the pages of this book.

Lastly, thank you to all who took the time to read chapters, join Morning Motivation Zooms and practice *flipping the switch* with me! Darkness can't exist in the light… Shine Bright my loves!

xo Joan

ABOUT
THE AUTHOR

Joan Robison is equal parts **business strategist, leadership coach, speaker, and trainer**. With a mission of igniting transformational change, Joan works with individuals and teams who want more. With kindness, insight, and coaching expertise, Joan helps people quickly *flip the switch* from a problem to a solution. She challenges others to become the people they are meant to be and to live a life they love.

Joan brings twenty years of experience as a top producer in network marketing. She has established and grown three multi-million dollar sales organizations. Joan views all that she does as a way of serving others, a mindset that started with her career in management at Nordstrom. Joan is known for her exceptional ability to develop and build leadership skills in others. She encourages others to rise by empowering them to be their best selves. Joan is a DSWA Certified Coach and Trainer who helps leaders and sales organizations improve their organizational growth and leadership development.

When Joan isn't working, you can find her hiking or climbing mountains in Arizona. She enjoys traveling and is always ready for the next adventure.

**To learn more about how Joan can help you
or your team reach the next level, visit:
www.joanrobison.com**

What was your *Flip The Switch* moment?
Share your feedback.
Read what others have to say.
Join the conversation!

What People Are Saying About *Flip The Switch*

www.joanrobison.com/WhatPeopleAreSaying
AboutFlipTheSwitch

WHAT PEOPLE
ARE SAYING ABOUT
FLIP THE SWITCH

From the very first few minutes you start reading Joan's book, you feel your life begin to transform. What would happen if you could *flip off the switch* of fear that keeps you frozen in your steps, and turn on the switch of love that keeps you growing and learning? You'll step into your light as you hear Joan's stories. She captures your imagination in a meaningful and mesmerizing way and you will be transported to a new place and time living a better life for yourself. So many of our decisions are driven by our fears, and once we can identify those and deal with them, new doors will open. Joan coaches you through each phase of your personal growth journey, with specific steps to transformation. I encourage you to take out a journal and do the exercises. Immerse yourself in the inquisition of your life and your personal growth will bring you a fresh new life that you love.

JORDAN ADLER
Author, Amazon Best Seller "Beach Money" and Network Marketing Dream Broker

Joan has hit an absolute home run with *Flip The Switch*! The wisdom around mindset alone in this book will have you performing at your absolute best to increase your impact on the world. It's simple, relatable and broken down gently so you can focus on implementing! Prepare for Joan's guidance to completely transform your life and business.

BRIAN FRYER
Coach Fryer

When I first met Joan, I saw her determination to make a difference in her own life, but especially in others. She proceeded to work on herself to become the precious child God intended her to be. I enjoyed many late night calls to discuss numerous issues along the way. She was always open to suggestions and of course I benefitted more by the end of a conversation. We've shared many lunches and coffees along the way. I've always walked away feeling blessed that God put Joan in my life. No doubt you will enjoy her book: *Flip The Switch*!

BOB TAYLOR
Life Counselor & Health Solutions

Flip The Switch is magnetic! It immediately focuses on getting your mind in the right place to create a successful future. If you are ready to change your perspective on business and truly flash forward to find success, this book is for you!

MARINA SIMONE
Network Marketing Top Coach

The only person you can change is yourself. When you change your mindset, your world will open you up to new possibilities and new adventures. Fortunately, you don't need to travel the path to a new fearless you by yourself. You can have Joan! Watching her grandfather and dad as they ran a store, Joan learned how to serve others. Later, at Nordstrom, she paid attention to the best salespeople. For the last 20 years, Joan has developed hundreds of leaders in network marketing. She is truly a "leader maker." If you want to lead your life and help others to do the same, read this book!

JAY LIESNER
President, Sylvina Consulting

Joan is as delightful and powerful on paper as she is in person. Her tips on word choice and the story we tell ourselves have the force to positively impact all aspects of our lives.

LANCE CONRAD
Entrepreneur, Investor, Success Strategist, Speaker

It's time! Time to take your whole "package" – all of you -- acknowledge yourself and all of the working parts you bring to each day; saute' with acceptance, elevate with a positive vibration, honor your fears, and move into life with a plan. We all need a plan. Some of us are webmasters and need a very loose/unstructured framework. Others can feed directly from these incredible specifics outlined in *Flip The Switch*, and move into the worthy life we all deserve!

IVALY ALEXANDER
Vice President, Scott Alexander's Golf, Inc.

Self-help books motivate me, but it never seems to stick. I'm one chapter into *Flip The Switch*, and it finally seems possible! If you are also struggling with mindset, I encourage you to *flip the switch*.

MOLLY FITCH
National Executive Director, Color Street

Flip The Switch is truly a game changer for your personal life and professional life. Joan has a fun and simple way of breaking down how to change your mindset that will impact your life for the better and help you make better choices along the way!

SHEILA CONLIN
Owner, The Conlin Company

What I particularly love about what Joan has done in *Flip The Switch* is how each chapter includes personal experiences, actual verbiage to use to help with the transition of mindset, activities that will make you reflect, dig deep and be honest with yourself, and self-coaching activities and questions. At the conclusion of each chapter, Joan encourages you to put what you have learned in action. The tips, advice and simple activities shared are a results of Joan's proven track record, having built three multi-million dollar organizations and coached thousands of people.

NANCY ROBINSON
Vice President Sales Leader, Norwex

I couldn't sleep last night as the stresses of the day, week, month were spinning in my head. I remembered **Flip The Switch** and knew it was time to start reading it. I can't wait to read more and share this book with my team.

HEIDI KAUFFMAN
Professional Equestrian Athlete, Mindset Coach, Author and Owner, Hillcrest Training LLC

Flip The Switch is a quick, easy read with solid concrete steps to get you "unstuck" in your business. She actually walks you through what to do! She is the best at what she does. I am lucky enough to have learned from the best!

CONNIE FEIKES
Founding Executive - H2O at Home

Joan is a no-nonsense leader! Her trainings get you and your team right into action. We all know the action is where the magic happens. So when Joan coaches or trains... I'm all eyes and ears!

KELLY KUCERA
National Executive Director, Color Street

In Joan Robison's book, **Flip The Switch**, she doesn't just tell stories. She gives you practical suggestions and strategies on how you, too, can **flip the switch** to make the necessary changes you need to make to live your best life! Mindset matters most and you'll understand why after reading this book!

TERESA EPPS
Certified Leadership Coach & Trainer

There is no doubt that this book is a gem. After just one chapter I have already made changes to my routine and mindset. So I am shouting out to all my entrepreneur friends and even my non-entrepreneur friends who are ready to level up life. This book will definitely help you find the focus you need to grow and be a better you and finally start living a life you love! You deserve that!

ERIN STONES
National Executive Director, Color Street

Joan Robison's book, *Flip The Switch*, is as inspirational as it is practical. Joan lovingly teaches you how you can manifest your best life by changing your thinking. I love that each chapter gives you self-coaching questions and then gives you action steps! This book is helpful in business and in your personal life. It should be on everyone's bookshelf. It would also make a great gift!

JANE NEUENSCHWANDER
Senior Director, Color Street

This book is definitely a recharge for me. It's filled with real life relatable content and speaks to those who want to be a better version of themselves!

ANDREA PAINE

After reading just a few pages of *Flip The Switch*, I had some amazing ideas on how to shift a couple things and it has made an amazing difference. This book is gold if you are needing to realize a transformation in your life and nothing seems to be working.

MANDY MCGOWAN
Multipreneur, Tax Practice Success

This book gives you easy, quick and applicable steps to take to develop a positive mindset that will impact every aspect of your life. Her tips can be implemented immediately, backed with the "why" we all want. Joan connects her teachings to tangible situations we can all connect to. I think everyone could benefit from reading this. I just read Chapter Two, and already I've started to find ways to implement her tips into my thinking. It takes practice, friends!

JEN MCCANN
CEO, JM Retail Services

Joan Robison's book is life-changing. I cannot wait for my friends and my team to get their hands on it!! I especially enjoy how she shares personal stories which helps me to relate. Her book gives me the tools to grow and experience my own personal development. I cannot wait for my friends, family, and team to get their hands on this book.

AMANDA BURT
Director, Color Street

If you're tired of being held back by fear or a negative mindset, this is the book for you. The first part of the book is filled with understanding where you are along with simple, doable steps to move you to where you want to be. Want to multiply your successes through this process? Being coached by Joan allowed me to get real with myself and feel like I was in a safe space. She's literally "been there" and is transparent in sharing her experiences and then gently guiding you through yours.

Suzie Read
Regional Sales Manager, Norwex

Joan is a great leader, always motivating, challenging, inspiring and genuine. She puts people first and has written a great book which can help anyone *flip the switch* on their mindset, grow their business, and circle of influence. It's a great read for anyone in business, leadership, direct sales or otherwise, as well as great motivation for the teenagers/college students in your life.

Amanda Hines
Accountant, Bookminders

Joan is the guru of coaches!! She drives the person she is working with to determine what they want to improve on, and she incorporates the skills that they already possess and combines them both. She helps to establish the new skills and incorporates daily accountability for consistency so that this specific skill set becomes a habit! She engages her clients by focusing on positive personal development, and her overall demeanor is as genuine as they come!

Lauren Marco
National Executive Director, Color Street

After working with Joan Robison for the past year, she has opened my eyes to what I feared. Through her coaching sessions, she has given me the tools to have a more positive outlook on life. She walked me through my fears to see they are just the thoughts I create. Before working with her, I never realized how fear can handcuff you from a life you have always wanted. I am so excited Joan has written this book to help others like she has helped me.

Kristie De Menna
Sapphire National Executive Director, Color Street

Joan's Morning Motivations are a priority for me and I rarely miss them. The breathing exercises that we do have been incorporated into so many areas of my life and enable me to *flip the switch* to a more pleasant state of mind and being. I also do a few every morning with my daughter and my 21 month-old granddaughter. Can't start too early. Cutest experience ever!!

TARIE MACMILLAN
Director, Color Street

While dealing with significant cleanup and loss from the recent Hurricane Ida flood, I have been able to smile and laugh. Joan taught me to see that I only need to do the next right thing to move forward, and that stuff is just stuff. Using the tools I have learned allows me to *flip the switch* and change my focus. When my focus is on gratitude and what is working in my life, I can really handle anything with focus, ease, and grace.

LAURA SHREVE
Team Leader, Color Street

Joan is an elite coach that forever changed my life. She is the leader of leaders! Working with Joan has helped me develop into the ultimate leader for my team. She will help you get to the core of any obstacle and be by your side to guide you through it.

MEGAN MILES
Senior Executive Director, Color Street

Joan Nilsen Robison has helped me over the years come through diversity and to see ALL circumstances in a positive way. You've heard it before, "We can't control outside influences, however, we can control how we choose to look at them and react to them. " Let's keep it real. This is easier said than done. It is a "practice" for sure. You must have tools you can plug into! Joan's new book, *Flip The Switch*, is seriously a game changer for everyone. If you are looking to change your situation, whether it's your business or the relationships in your life, this is a must read!

TRACEY VLAHOS
Chief Sales officer at EverraOfficial

Joan's coaching the past year and a half has helped transform me into the more confident, more goal oriented, less of a people pleaser, leader that I am today. Joan transforms people's lives, both professionally and personally!

SHARON SUTLIFF
Senior Director, Color Street

Joan has helped me reframe the definition of "overwhelmed." I now see it this way: "The Lord has given you so much of exactly what you asked for so fast, and you're having a hard time processing it all so quickly." When you change the way you think, the way you feel changes too. When I feel overwhelmed, I now smile and thank the Lord for my fullness!

HOLLY CARSON
Team Leader, Color Street

Now more than ever people need great tools like this book to help them overcome fear and to live their best lives. Joan is a living inspiration of how anyone can create anything they want in life by simply changing their mindset and going to work on themselves!

CAREY CONLEY
Speaker, Author and Vision Expert

I can hear Joan's voice in the words of **Flip The Switch**. The Total Mindset Reboot comes at a perfect time! The self-coaching questions are a great accountability check with myself.

ANITA WESTLAKE
Senior Executive Director & Presidential Circle Member, Color Street

I read an early chapter of Joan's new book, **Flip The Switch**. It was exactly what I needed to hear to reframe my mindset. Joan is a treasure. If personal development and leveling up is your thing, check it out!

AMBER SPENCE
Sapphire National Executive, Presidential Team Member, Color Street

Monday & Friday mornings begin with a Zoom gathering of emotionally & professionally supportive individuals, hosted by Joan Robison. Even when I wake-up severely depressed, meditation, other's stories & the inspiration allows me to change my focus. I am then able to accomplish something with my day rather than staying in bed & crying! These meetings and these individuals have saved my life.

ROBERTA SANTA CROCE
Stylist, Color Street

Joan is real, raw, and genuine. Her desire to help others is evident in all that she does. I love partaking in all that she has to offer any chance I get!

CODI BILLS
Sapphire National Executive Director, Color Street

Reading the second chapter of *Flip The Switch*, and realizing how my thoughts and beliefs and thoughts have so much control over my mindset, was so impactful. Mindset is the key to anything that we keep locked in this life. Joan shows us how we look at situation is a choice, and offers tools on how to put the practices into action.

BRITTNEY METTKE POWERS
Ruby National Executive Director and Presidential Team member, Color Street

Joan always has the most thoughtful and intuitive words to share, and her unique perspective is loud and clear in *Flip The Switch*. Instead of telling you what to do, Joan guides you through how to do by making changes to the words you say to yourself and using logic to balance your emotions. When you make the mindset changes as Joan suggests, it frees you from otherwise negative and distracting emotions so you can reach your goals and potential.

ASHLYN MILLANG
Senior Executive Director & Presidential Circle Member, Color Street

When I was treated to a sneak peek of Joan's new book, I particularly loved this: "Think of strengthening your mindset the way you think of building muscles at the gym. As you practice fostering your mindset, be good to yourself. It takes time, commitment, and practice. Each step you take will build endurance, and endurance is what will separate you from the pack." If you are looking to grow yourself, your relationships or your business you'll love *Flip The Switch*.

RISA GARRETT
Senior Executive Director, Color Street

Yes! Joan supported to simplify & prioritize to abundantly grow in goals and dreams! She is amazing at asking engaging questions to get you to think at a higher level and breaking though stuck mindset!

MARIAN FORREST
Independent Sales Director, Mary Kay

Not only is Joan a fantastic coach, she is a badass example of a woman I aspire to be.

MONICA ARCE
Independent National Executive Director & Presidential Circle Member, Color Street

I literally devoured Joan Nilsen Robison's book, *Flip The Switch*, and frequently found myself teary-eyed while reading. So much of it hits home for me. This book provides the exact steps you can take in order to move forward in this challenging time as well as future ones. No matter where you are in life and/or your career, there is so much to learn in Joan's book.

JENNIFER KUPIEC
Director, Color Street

This is a must read!!! Joan take on mindset and energy really hit home with me!!! You can tell she's passionate about what she's sharing. I believe she will help you *flip the switch* in your life from fear to joy.

CHAMI MORGAN

Joan has been a partner and a friend, helping me through some of the biggest obstacles in my business and my personal life. Because of her, I get to take what she has taught me and make a huge impact in the world by being a better person, leader, and mother. The world is also a better place because of her.

ALLYSON ALONZO
Senior Executive Director, Color Street

I have had the pleasure of working alongside Joan Robison for a few years, and she has had an incredible impact on me. Joan has the ability to help you transform a problem/situation you may be struggling with, and find a solution. Her outlook on every challenge has helped me overcome some of my biggest obstacles. Joan is the mentor we all need in our life!!

ESSIE PRIGGE
Owner, Blush & Cactus Boutique

I can't tell you how excited I am about *Flip The Switch*. I met Joan Nilsen Robison earlier this year and fell in love with her drive, work ethic, wit and passion for life.

ALYSSA COWART
Owner, Alyssa M. Cowart

Joan Nilsen Robison has spent the last 20 years supporting and training people on how to live their best lives, how to overcome the things that hold us back, and how our mindset is where it all starts. I got a sneak peek at *Flip The Switch*, and OMG.

JODI MINKER
Senior Director, Color Street

Without a doubt, *Flip The Switch* is next level wealth of information. Whether you're in business, or simply into self-improvement, dive into the magic that fills the pages. This book is a fantastic reference guide, and I will unashamedly be quoting bits and pieces from it in my conversations going forward.

MALVIKA SHERMAN

I am so excited to see Joan's book come to life. It has a great message and tangibles you can implement. Five stars!

TONI VANSCHOYCK
Director & Five Million Dollar Income Club

Flip The Switch is a great reminder how my mindset can have a positive impact on my life and those I interact with both personally and professionally. I love the focus on living intentionally and with high vibrations and the tools provided are easy and actionable.

ANNA CANEPA-SMITH
Director, Business Continuity

When Joan and I first connected, I knew she was a talent in the industry. When Joan shared the concept of *Flip The Switch* and her book, I loved it! Joan provides empowering strategies that you can implement right away to change your business, life and mind. Enjoy your read and watch your life change.

SAM CHURCH
Six-figure online business owner and world traveler

Joan is a masterful leader and coach! I have worked with her as a coaching client and by utilizing the steps she taught me my business grew exponentially!

MARONDA GARZONE
Small Business Owner, Consider it DONE Your Personal Concierge Service

Needing a change in your life but don't know where to begin? Ready to take action, but don't know what to do? Joan will lead you through the misconceptions of life to an intention plan to transform you to live the life you were meant to live!

KIMBERLY HESS
Speaker, Trainer, Coach John Maxwell Team Member

Flip The Switch is the ideal book during a time in history when fear of control, uncertainty and the unknown is evident in our world. Joan Robison shows us how to live in light and how that expands all possibility. So grateful for *Flip The Switch*!

STEVE WILTSHIRE

CEO & Founder, Steve Wiltshire - Lifeline Coaching & Education, Inc.

I am so very fortunate for Joan and our weekly morning motivation and grounding calls. I have learned so much. I can utilize her amazing tools in all aspects of my life.

TASHALEIGH RYERSON

Team Leader, Color Street

When I learned that Joan had written a book about her life experiences and how you can *flip the switch*, I knew I wanted to read it. Reading just one preview chapter, Joan has inspired me to live to my full potential. Looking forward to reading the rest of the book and following her on her exciting journey!

MINDY SAUNDERS

Co-owner, Mindy and Mandy

Joan is real and inspirational making her an outstanding coach and leader. Her ability to guide and challenge people stands out above others making her an exceptional coach.

MAAREN STROBLE

Independent Consultant, PartyLite

Working with Joan has given me such peace through the inner knowing that the only thing I can control is myself and how I react to any situation. She has helped me to always be looking for the lesson in everything. When you're always seeking answers life feels more like a game.

HEATHER ENGELSMAN

Senior Executive Director, Color Street

I have grown so much in my life and business since working with Joan. Her content is so powerful for mind body and soul.

DENA LUEDTKE
Senior Director, Color Street

Joan is a master at getting people to recognize their own gifts, and she personalizes a path to get you where you want to be. She believes in you so much that you can't help but believe in yourself!

ANDREA DUNBAR
Director, Color Street

Joan's 20 years of experience in helping others makeover their mindset has empowered hundreds of women to reach their goals. In this book she helps you intentionally focus on your mindset so you can elevate your life and others. *Flip The Switch* will give you the hope and help you need to take charge of your own thoughts & actions.

KELLI FRANCE
CEO of Fear LESS Girl Co.

Treat yourself to the gift of Joan's life experiences. You just might see there's so much waiting for you when you *flip the switch*. With vulnerability, Joan provides a practical framework for stepping into your light.

KELLI JOCHUM

Joan has been a major contributor in helping me clearly define my priorities to live my life by design. Her willingness and determination to share her knowledge and help others succeed is a passion that sets her above all others. I highly recommend Joan for anyone who wants to thrive!

TRACILEA YOUNG
Advocate and Presidential Founder, Green Compass Global

Joan Robison motivates beautifully in this book by speaking from her heart, delivering powerful personal stories that drive home her easy to learn strategies she has developed with a vast amount of experience. This is a must-read with solid action steps for entrepreneurs and anyone looking to improve their perspective on life. Bravo, Joan!

ANN BRODETTE
Regional Director

Joan has walked the walk, so she can talk the talk! I was floating in a cloud of negativity. As I implemented Joan's tools, I have become more positive in my thinking. As a result, I am finding a whole new happiness within myself!

DEBBIE HOSELTON
Senior Stylist, Color Street

Inspiring! Instructional Empowering! *Flip The Switch* makes you believe you can live the life you want to live, and it shows you how. Joan takes you on a self-improvement journey that will help you out massively.

FRAZER BROOKES
Author, I Dare You

This book had me at hello! As an avid reader, I was grateful for the gems of wisdom and golden insights Joan delivered. Before you dive into *Flip the Switch*, be sure to have a highlighter in hand!

GRACE KEOHOHOU HAO
Co-Founder of Coach Excellence School

CPSIA information can be obtained
at www.ICGtesting.com
Printed in the USA
FSHW022323121221